*That Book in the Attic*

# That Book in the Attic

by Helen K. Oswald

Pacific Press Publishing Association

Mountain View, California
Omaha, Nebraska

PACIFIC
PRESS
PUB.
ASSN.

PRINTED
IN U·S·A·

*Contents*

# 1

# The Strange Visitor

The air was full of music. The birds had returned, and their songs were as welcome as the bright, warm spring sunshine.

"Come on, boys, get along!" It was father's voice from across the fields as he encouraged the horses at their work. From another direction we could hear my brother Henry's young voice lustily chiming in with the music nature had provided. He often sang as he worked in the expansive and fertile fields of our old home in the southern part of South Dakota.

Fourteen children were born into this home on the prairies—and a happy home it was. Well do I remember how, each morning after breakfast, we would all sit around the long family table until father had read a portion of Scripture. Then we would stand with folded hands and bowed heads while he prayed for the welfare of his family. After father's "Amen" all the children recited the Lord's Prayer in chorus.

After the evening meal we again remained seated around the table and waited for father to start a hymn. When father gave the pitch, everyone, no matter how tired, would join in singing. After two or three hymns father said "Good night" to the younger children, who then scampered off to bed. Mother followed to see that each one was tucked in for the night. Each child was taught to kneel beside his bed and say a short prayer. While mother was busy with the younger children, my two elder sisters washed the supper dishes. Father scanned the newspaper as I knelt before him with a basin of water and washed his dusty, tired feet. Soon we would all be off to bed.

On Sunday, if our parents drove away to visit a church in the neighborhood, some of us were always allowed to go along. The rest of the children entertained themselves at home. When we did not go to church, we would have Sunday school at home. Each one had to learn to read the Bible and memorize some texts. We were not allowed to play rough games on Sunday; we were taught that it was a sacred day, and that we were to be quiet and reverent.

Father was always careful about our associates. He would not tolerate rough language. If we used slang or tried to deceive in any way, we were punished.

We all had to work hard on the farm, and each one's work was carefully outlined for the day. On this particular spring morning, with the work divided and assigned, father took his four horses to a field to put in the last acres of grain. Henry had gone to another field with two horses and a walking plow to start plowing for corn. My eldest sister, Mary, had to do the housework and care for the baby, and my second eldest sister, Katie, had to herd the cattle.

My work was to help mother plant the garden, which Henry had plowed early in the morning. Mother sat down by the gate to select the seeds she wanted to put in first. I started to smooth the ground with the rake while she was arranging her seeds.

"Mother, what makes the seeds grow into plants?" I asked in childish sincerity.

"The seeds must die, dear, in order for them to grow," mother responded.

"The seeds must die in order to grow!" I pondered this statement, but it was too deep for me to grasp.

2

I was still wondering how the seeds must die in order to live, when I was startled by the jumping and desperate barking of our old dog down toward the creek. When I looked up, I saw a strange man approaching. Mother had gone into the house to feed the baby, and I was frightened. The railroad ran only a half mile to the east, and often transients would come to our house for food. They were sometimes discourteous.

I did not want this man to know I was frightened, so I kept right on working, pretending I was unafraid. "This man must be different," I thought, for the dog quieted down and walked behind him, wagging his tail as though he had found a friend. Instead of going to the house, the man came straight for the garden. He put his little grip down and leaned on the gate as though he were very tired.

"Good morning, little lady!" he said cheerfully. "That is nice work you are doing. Do you believe your garden will grow?"

"I think it will," I answered, still frightened.

"Isn't this a beautiful day?" he said. "God gives the beautiful sunshine; and, if He sends rain, the garden will surely grow. Do you know the different seeds?" he asked with a smile.

I moved closer and closer to the gate as I showed him the seeds I had. Soon I lost all fear, for he talked about God and told me that the seeds would have to die in the ground in order to bring forth fruit—the same thing mother had told me.

The man put his hand on my head and said, "God bless you, little girl. If you are a good girl, God will help you to grow and become strong so you can do many kind deeds in this life; and after this life, God will give you a home in heaven." He had such a kind voice and friendly eyes that I stood speechless as he spoke.

The stranger said he was thirsty, so we started to the house for a drink. Mother was shocked to find a strange man standing in the doorway with me. After quenching his thirst, he told his mission—selling Christian literature. He showed her his books; but mother said she could not buy any unless

**3**

father agreed. She told him that father would be home for dinner, and if he came back to have dinner with us, he would have a chance to show the books to father.

Our visitor hurried off to see two of the nearest neighbors, later coming back for dinner. Father received him kindly. We children hoped with all our hearts that father would buy one of those interesting books, and we almost shouted for joy when he ordered one. We watched for weeks for the man to return.

One rainy summer day toward evening he returned with *Daniel and the Revelation,* the book father had ordered. We looked carefully at all the pictures in it. We children were too young to understand much of the message it contained, but father read some of it. After a time he discovered that the book said something about Sabbath observance, declaring that the seventh day is the Sabbath of God.

Father exclaimed with amazement, "This is a deceptive book!" Fearing the family would be misled by it, he hid it away in the attic, unbeknown to us.

For a long time none of us knew where it was. Whenever mother and father were gone any length of time, we would search the house for that book. We wanted to look at the pictures. For months we did not find it. Then one day my eldest brother, Henry, said, "There is only one place left where it might be—the attic."

There was no stairway to the attic; so at his suggestion we ran to get a stepladder. Together we got it upstairs and pushed its nose into the two-foot-square opening in the ceiling. Henry climbed up and was there for some minutes before we heard the happy shout, "I've found it! I've found it!" We all shouted for joy. He climbed down in a hurry. We rushed into the living room, and there placed the book on the floor. We lay down on the floor, and each one tried to get his head closest. After we had looked it through two or three times, we returned it to the attic. Many of the pictures were a puzzle to us, and we talked much about what they might mean; however, we were always careful that father did not hear us.

I often wondered how that book could be so bad; many of the pictures it contained were Bible pictures, and the book had been sold to us by such a kind Christian man.

One day father and I were doing some work together in a field about four miles from home. We could not drive home for dinner, for it was too much of a trip for tired horses; so we took our lunch along. After we had eaten, father lay down under the wagon for a short nap. I entertained myself by looking at the pictures on the paper in which our lunch had been wrapped. There I saw a picture of a man who looked like the kind man who had sold father that book.

When father awoke, I told him about the picture. This prompted father to talk at length about the strange doctrines that were in the book. He said he had often heard about a church that kept Saturday and taught about strange animals, such as lions and leopards with wings, and a great red dragon; but he had never seen one of these people until this agent came. Of course he did not know what denomination the man represented when he purchased the book.

"Well, I think the man was a good man," I said, "and I hope he will visit us again."

I often looked down the road and wished that man would come again and talk as kindly to me as he had talked that spring morning, but he never returned.

## 2

# Baby Brother "Goes to Heaven"

About one-thirty one morning I awoke with the queerest feeling—a feeling that something was wrong. I thought I could hear sobs. I got up and tiptoed down the dark stairs to see what was happening. As I opened the door to the living room, I saw mother kneeling beside the baby's crib. She was weeping.

"Mother, what is the matter?" I asked, putting my arm around her. She said that baby brother was very ill; she was afraid he would die. Father had gone for the doctor. I saw that our baby was burning with fever, and his breathing was rapid.

I went out and listened for sounds of father's return with the doctor; but all was still. The doctor lived many miles away, the roads were poor, and the heavy farm horses could not travel fast.

About daybreak we could hear them coming, and we were relieved; we felt sure that the doctor would be able to help the baby. But, alas, father returned alone! The doctor was sick in bed and could not make the trip. However, he had sent some medicine.

After mother had given the baby some of the medicine, he seemed to rest easier, but the next day toward evening he grew worse. We children retired at bedtime, but mother sat up to watch and do what she could. Father stayed close by to help. Before the next dawn, baby died.

It was indeed sad to lose little brother from our home. We all loved him, and he had been such a ray of sunshine that the home did not seem the same for months after he had gone. We often looked into the empty cradle and wept. Our parents tried to comfort us by saying that the baby had gone to heaven and was now an angel.

One evening mother and I were sitting in the yard waiting for father to come home from a neighbor's, where he had been helping for two days. As we saw the stars coming out brightly one by one, mother remarked that they were little windows in heaven, and that the angels could look through and watch us. This impressed me, and I wondered which might be the bright window my dear little brother was using to look down on us.

There were many things that puzzled me, and I wanted to ask many questions. But I knew I was wearying mother; so I kept my thoughts to myself. Somehow I couldn't understand why they put our baby into a coffin and then into another box and buried him in that deep grave if he had gone to heaven. I kept wondering and wondering about this, but for a long time it remained a mystery to me.

One day father and I were driving slowly past the cemetery where baby brother was buried. I could not restrain the tears as I saw the weeping willow tree that gently waved its graceful branches over brother's grave.

"I know, little girl," father softly said, trying to comfort me. "You must not cry, though, for baby brother is happy in heaven."

This started all that perplexity surging again in my mind. I could not hold back the questions any longer. "Why did you bury baby in that coffin in that deep grave if he was going to heaven? If Jesus wanted another angel, why didn't He take baby from home before you put him in that dark hole? Did the angels take off all the dirt so Jesus could get brother out of the grave and carry him to heaven? And why does mother cry when she visits the grave with flowers if baby is not there at all?"

Father sighed, and put his strong arm around me. Then he said, "Baby's body is still in the grave, Helen, but his soul is in heaven."

"What is the soul?" was the next question.

Father's arm tightened as he drew me close to his side and said, "Don't worry about those things now, dear  You are too young to understand. Someday when you grow up, it will all become plain to you; and, if you are a good girl, you will one day be up there with baby and the other angels." This thought made me happy, and I felt satisfied with father's explanation.

The months passed by, and one morning after worship father said, "Well, the time has come for the three elder children to go to confirmation school." I did not know why that had to be, but I thought it must be a good thing if father desired it. For about six weeks they were away from home, attending a Bible school conducted by a minister.

On the Sunday morning when they, with about twenty other students, were confirmed, I was permitted to go to church with our parents to attend the service. The rostrum was decorated with greenery and pink roses. The boys were all dressed in new dark suits, and they occupied the rear row of chairs on the rostrum. The girls were dressed in white and sat in an orderly row in front of the boys. It was the prettiest program I had ever seen.

After a few songs were sung and prayer had been offered, the minister asked many questions, to which his confirmation class responded with texts that had been memorized. I thought it was wonderful to be able to study the Bible so that one could repeat so much of it from memory.

"When may I be confirmed?" I asked father on the way home from church.

8

"In a year or two," he replied. That sounded like a long time; but I accepted the fact that father knew best, and so I dismissed it from my mind.

The following Monday morning father said the pastures were becoming dry and the cattle were not getting enough to eat. Pointing to me, he said, "Helen, it will be your job for a number of weeks to take the cattle down to the lake where there is good grazing, and to watch them so that they will not get into the neighbors' fields." I took my pony and dog and began my job. The days seemed long. Presently a happy thought came to me. "If only I could have that nice big book out here with me, it would be a wonderful pastime."

I managed to get it out of the attic one evening. After carefully wrapping it in paper, I carried it to a stone pile I passed each day with the cattle. Every morning I would get off my horse, get the book, and then take it with me into the fields for the day.

For weeks I read it—every word of it. But summer was soon past, and it was time to get ready for school. Soon the book found its place again in the attic.

# 3

# Why We Got No Bibles

My younger brother, Leonhard, and I had a good time attending school during winter. In the spring father and mother went away for a few days to visit relatives. During this visit father became acquainted with a minister to whom he took a liking.

"I have two children who should be confirmed," father told him.

"Fine! Send them to me, and I will confirm them with the young people of my church," said the minister.

Father and mother were quite pleased with the idea. They immediately made arrangements for Leonhard and me to stay with relatives during the six weeks.

It took us nearly all day to drive the twenty-five miles to Uncle John's home. Father stayed overnight to let the horses rest, as they were very tired. And we were glad he stayed, for everything was strange; this was the first time we had been so far away from home, and we were homesick already. The next morning before daybreak father started back.

At nine o'clock the ringing of the church bell called all the confirmation students to the church. There were twenty-three in all. We started our work the first day by learning some songs and repeating the Lord's Prayer; then we had to read a few Bible chapters. The second day we memorized John 3:16, along with some other texts and a poem about clean hearts and clean hands. The third day the catechism was introduced. From its pages we had to memorize quotations from the church fathers, the Ten Commandments as the catechism had them recorded, and some other passages.

All went well until one day something was said about the soul. I well remembered how bewildered my mind was on that topic after my brother died and father told me that I should understand it better when I grew older. A number of years had now passed, and I thought my mind could grasp anything now; it surely would not be out of place to ask the minister for an explanation of the puzzling question. In all sincerity I asked courteously, "Please, will you tell us what is the soul?"

Turning to me, he inquired, "Why do you ask that question?"

"Because I do not understand it, and I wish it explained," I replied.

"I will talk to you after school!" This was his only answer. Some of the students laughed. I thought no doubt he wanted to explain it to me alone, so I was satisfied with his response.

At four o'clock school was dismissed. I remained until all the students had gone. The minister called me to the front and gave me a chair near his desk. I sat down. All was quiet for a moment; then came the words: "Why did you ask me that question this afternoon?"

"Because I do not understand what the soul is, and I am anxious to have it explained," I told him again.

He then told me that he would not try to explain such questions, and that henceforth I should keep my questions to myself. With that he dismissed me.

I was shocked almost to tears. I took my books and hat and started to leave. When I reached the door, most of the students were in the entry waiting to shame me for having to stay after school. I was much chagrined. I went straight to

**11**

my room and did not eat any supper. Late into the night I tried to figure out what could have been wrong with my question and why the minister took the attitude he did. But I found no solution. I wished I could talk the matter over with my parents; but they were twenty-five miles away, and there was no one else who would understand. Morning came at last. I tried not to let my uncle and aunt see that I was fighting a hard battle in my mind and heart.

Leonhard knew I felt hurt, but he did not say a word until after breakfast, when we were on our way to school. "You feel bad because you had to stay after school, don't you, Helen?"

"Yes," I told him. Brother was sympathetic and tried to comfort me in my perplexity. The day passed smoothly except for the unkind remarks some of the students made at recess.

One morning the minister told us there was only one more week left before confirmation. Further, he said every one of us who could say he was converted by Saturday night would receive a beautiful Bible on the Sunday morning when confirmation took place. I wanted to ask him the meaning of the word "conversion," for I had no idea what it meant; but I did not dare, for fear it would cause trouble again.

The week passed quickly, for we worked diligently on our memory work so we would be sure not to make mistakes on the day when our parents and friends and many other people would be in church to see us confirmed. During the week, the students stood up one by one and said with tears, "I am converted."

Friday noon, on the way home from school, brother asked, "Helen, are you converted yet?"

"I don't think so," I answered.

"Well, at recess time," Leonhard said, "I asked some of the boys who had said they were converted how they got that way, and they said they just cried and prayed until they saw Jesus on the cross or until they saw an angel or some great light. They said that was a sign that one was converted."

Neither Leonhard nor I had gone through any such experience, but we did so want the Bibles. We thought it would be wonderful to have Bibles all our own. In our home only father had one.

"What can bring this experience into our lives?" we asked each other. But we could find no answer; we had never even prayed by ourselves, save for the simple bedtime prayer mother had taught us.

I was thirteen years old, and Leonhard was not quite twelve. We decided to go to brother's room after supper and cry and pray until we saw something similar to what the others said they had seen. We did not dare to make too much noise, for fear someone might hear us. Both of us tried to cry and pray; but somehow we did not get anywhere. We could not even shed one honest tear! We felt rather ashamed of ourselves as we looked at each other. Soon we became tired and went to our studies.

So the next morning at school the question remained un-settled. On the way home at noon, we talked the matter over. We decided not to say we were converted when we had not had the experience some of the students said they had. We would rather lose the much-coveted Bibles than to lie and get the Bibles dishonestly.

The afternoon was a busy one. We rehearsed and rehearsed until it looked as if our program Sunday morning would be presented perfectly. We were dismissed at suppertime. After supper we took our baths and washed our hair. We were anxious for the next morning to arrive, for our parents and some of our brothers and sisters were to come. They were also to bring the new clothes that were to be worn on the great occasion.

Our folks did not arrive until about nine o'clock Sunday morning, although they had left home at midnight and should have been there early. One of the horses had taken sick on the road. When at last they did arrive, we hurried into our new clothes and ran. We did not have time to tell the folks that we were not receiving Bibles with the others, or the reason why.

I was very happy about my pretty white dress. It had many

13

tucks and ruffles, plus lace and a pretty silk sash. Brother's new dark-brown suit just matched his handsome brown eyes. He had a pink rosebud in his coat lapel, and I wore three little pink roses in my hair. We arrived at church on time and rehearsed the hardest parts once more before the congregation began to gather.

Soon the doors opened, and the people began to fill every available space. At the appointed time, the organist began to play, and we marched in to our places. The minister came in and stood at the pulpit. Then we all sat down together. The program went off very well until the minister distributed the Bibles. We did not dare to manifest our feelings, for we were facing all the people. Our parents, of course, did not understand what it was all about.

After the meeting was dismissed, we hastily gathered our few belongings and started home. Because of the sick horse, we had to drive slowly. The first few miles little was said. Our parents were always very careful not to make remarks that would shake our confidence in anyone, and especially in a minister or a teacher; therefore they thought long before they commented about the experience of the day.

"Well, children, why didn't you receive Bibles today?" father finally asked. After we told him the reason, he said, "I am glad you were honest and did not act a lie in order to get the Bibles. I would rather have you slighted in the presence of all that congregation than to have such a sin marked against you in the books of heaven, for you would have to meet it in the judgment."

Mother echoed his statement by adding, "Yes, we are proud of you children because you were truthful. The angels wrote that in the book in which all your good deeds are recorded."

Leonhard and I had been close chums from babyhood. We were always glad to be in each other's company. The terrible accident that came to him one day during that following summer drew us even closer as I stayed by his bedside much of the time to comfort and cheer him.

At the beginning of harvest father promised that if we all

worked hard until the grain was cut he would give some money to each of us. This promise put us in good spirits, for we seldom went to town or had any money; and bananas, oranges, and candy were seen in our home only on holidays such as Easter, Christmas, and the Fourth of July.

One morning father, Henry, and Leonhard drove four miles to help our neighbor thresh. They were gone several days. Rainy weather set in one night; so they could not start work the next morning. While the men sat around and visited, Leonhard and the neighbor boy his age played by themselves in the hayloft. There they found an old shotgun. Accidentally the gun went off and shot Leonhard in the face. Father hastened to the doctor with him, but his eyelids had turned purple and were so swollen that it was impossible to examine them. He was then brought home. We feared he would die before morning, but he lived.

One morning, after everyone was out of the room, I put my face close to his ear and said, "I love you, brother; I am sorry you have to suffer so much."

He lifted his hand and touched my face. Then he began to cry. He wanted to say something, but his tongue was still terribly swollen, and he could not speak.

Another time it was my privilege to stay with him again. As I told him all the pleasant things I could think of, I could see traces of smiles around his mouth at times. This cheered me greatly, for I was sure now that he would get well. "Brother, I am so glad God spared your life," I said. "After you are well enough to get out of bed and kneel down, we will try to pray so that we can get converted, won't we?" He nodded in affirmation.

The doctor treated Leonhard's eyes each day to reduce the swelling so that he could pull the lids apart enough to admit light. Finally the day came when he could test the right eye. To our joy, brother could see, although the sight of his left eye was gone. He often said, "I am so thankful my life was spared and that I have one eye left!" His face did not look the same

15

after the accident, but I loved him even more when I saw some of his young friends shun him because his face was disfigured.

We did not lose our desire to become converted. One Sunday when our parents and the other children were attending church on the invitation of a neighbor, Leonhard said, "Now is our chance to pray while we are alone. Let's see if we can get converted."

We prayed and we prayed, but we did not ask forgiveness of our sins. We asked only to see something. We had not come to the place where we felt our need of a Saviour. We did not know that we needed one, but we wanted to experience something.

Finally we grew tired of praying, so Leonhard said, "Get that big book and read to me from it." I had been reading only a short time when we heard the folks return; so we hastily hid the book.

# 4

## The Lure of Worldly Pleasures

As we children grew into young manhood and young womanhood, we began to associate with other young people of the neighborhood. At first they would come and spend Sunday afternoon at our home, where we would play games while our parents sat and looked on.

George, my special friend, taught me to dance. At first my conscience hurt me a bit about dancing; but soon that feeling left, and I began to enjoy it greatly. George was a fine young man. He did not smoke, drink, or use vulgar language, as some young people did. My parents admired him, too; he was talented in many ways and was quite well-to-do.

With my new associations and interests, the world began to look inviting to me. My religious convictions faded. Noticing this, father and mother decided to take us to church oftener. However, we no longer enjoyed the church services as we once had, and some of the church members disapproved of our dancing. Brother Leonhard and I drifted somewhat apart, as he did not care for worldly entertainments and I greatly enjoyed them. I began to go more with Katie, my sister two years older than I, for she enjoyed the pleasures that I did.

One hot summer day father came home from the field with severe chills. He became very ill and was bedfast for a number of weeks. When he finally grew better and could be up, complications set in, and he developed rheumatic fever. His hands, legs, and feet swelled badly, and he suffered such intense pain that someone had to stay by his bedside day and night. Somehow I had always enjoyed doing something for anyone who was suffering; so, when all the rest were tired, I was happy to step in and try to make him comfortable. He appreciated my care and asked me to stay with him nights. I would go to bed early in the evening and sleep until mother was ready to retire. Then I would get up and wait on father until morning.

About two o'clock one morning father said, "Helen, I think I am going to die. I shall be glad to go, for I am tired of this pain." The tears rolled down his cheeks. I stood beside him and wiped them away, for he could not raise a hand. Every joint was stiff, and every movement he made was extremely painful. Although I did not want to grieve him, I soon broke down and wept with him.

Seeing my tears, father said, "Don't cry for me, my child. Rather, cry for yourself."

His breath was so short that I feared he was dying, and I did not want him to die with that statement on his lips. Mother, hearing my sobs, hurried downstairs. We gave him some medicine to steady his nerves and stimulate his heart. He slept soundly until daybreak but was weak the following day.

Father seemed so much better the next night that I ventured to ask him, "Father, what did you mean by saying 'Don't cry for me; rather, cry for yourself'?"

"Helen," said father kindly, "you have now grown to be a young woman, and I see a ring on your finger which George no doubt gave you. He is a fine young man, but he has led you into amusements that are sinful. I do not approve of them. It would be better for you to weep over these sins in your life than to weep for me."

Although I resolved at the time father was ill that I would not do anything to grieve my parents, as soon as father was well again, I forgot my good intentions. Soon I was having as good a time as ever.

Mother asked me one day, "Helen, don't you have any more desire to do right?"

"Yes, mother," I replied, "but I do not know where to turn for pastime. I don't enjoy going to church, for the people there are not cordial to us. Besides, there is plenty of time to have a little fun before I have to settle down, be sober, and prepare for death."

My sister felt even less inclined to give up these amusements than I did; so we drifted on.

One afternoon as father, Katie, and I were out in the field putting up hay, heavy clouds began to cover the western sky. It had been a hot day, and at first we welcomed the change in the atmosphere. Soon we could hear the deep thunder roll and see the lightning flash. Father called to us to unhitch our horses quickly. He said, "I fear a bad storm is coming; we must hurry home before it overtakes us."

A severe storm came. The dust was driven with such force that it became almost as dark as night. The flashes of lightning frightened the horses. Father had a hard time making the last half mile home, and we arrived just as the worst of the storm struck the farm. Father knew that mother would be frightened alone in the house with the little ones, so he jumped off the wagon and ran to the house. Katie and I managed to get the horses into the barn.

The storm grew so bad that we could not get to the house. The thunder and flashes of lightning were terrible. Neither of us said a word, but we thought much. I feared that the lightning might strike us, or the barn blow down upon us. Silently I began to ask God to spare our lives, and under my breath I partly promised I would change my ways and be good if He saved us from harm. I finally told Katie that I felt sure I would be lost should I perish in that storm, and I

**19**

wondered whether or not it was wise to wait until we were old before becoming Christians. While we were talking thus, the storm began to subside and a beautiful rainbow appeared. What a relief! The sun began to shine brightly, and everything looked beautiful and clean.

In the evening George came to call on me. He feared we had suffered harm because the worst of the storm had passed directly over our home. He said he and his brothers had watched it. He brought a number of other friends along, and we had a pleasant evening together. Before he went home, he told me what a big day the next Sunday was to be at their house, and he said he would come to get me if I would promise to go. In my heart there was a terrible conflict going on. I wanted to live up to my silent vow, made in the barn when the storm was raging, yet I did not have courage to say so. The temptation was so great that I accepted his invitation.

# 5

# To Church in a Tent

"What kind of show is going to be put on in that tent pitched over there on the corner?" asked father of a bystander one Sunday when he was in town.

"Well," laughingly answered the man, "it will be a different show from what anyone expects; it will be a religious show. Three young preachers are going to conduct meetings there, and they are so holy that they will not shake hands with anyone for fear they will become contaminated with sin!"

At suppertime father told us about the tent in town and what strange people were going to have a meeting that night. We were all eyes and ears. "Would you like to go?" he asked.

In a chorus we answered, "Yes!"

The dishes were quickly washed and the team hitched up. When we arrived in town, a friend of father's called out, "Where are you going with that load of people?"

"We are going to visit the meeting in the tent," father cheerfully called back.

"Well, they may be strange people," said another, "but they surely can sing well! They have been singing for about half an hour, and their songs are very good."

Father drove to a hitching post and tied up the team; then we all started for the tent. A large crowd had gathered about the tent. Some seemed to be afraid to go inside, some were talking about what they had heard about these people, and others were laughing.

As we reached the entrance of the tent, I saw two young men, a young woman, and a middle-aged couple standing on the rostrum singing. A deep hush came over me. Never before had I experienced anything like it. It seemed that I had stepped onto holy ground. We went in quietly and sat down on the very last seat near the entrance.

After the opening song, the middle-aged man asked the congregation to remain standing while prayer was offered. He knelt down beside that crude pulpit and prayed most earnestly. After the prayer one of the young men sang that beautiful song, "The Ninety and Nine."

> There were ninety and nine that safely lay
>     In the shelter of the fold,
> But one was out on the hills away,
>     Far, far from the gates of gold—
> Away on the mountains wild and bare,
>     Away from the tender Shepherd's care.
>
> "Lord, Thou hast here Thy ninety and nine;
>     Are they not enough for Thee?"
> But the Shepherd made answer: "One of Mine
>     Has wandered away from Me,
> And although the road be rough and steep,
>     I go to the desert to find My sheep."

At once I began to sense my lost condition. My heart began to press up into my throat until it seemed I would choke. The tears came. I tried to check them, but they kept coming. I felt I was that lost sheep of whom the young man was singing so earnestly. By the time he had finished the second stanza, I could hardly control my sobs. I did not want anyone to know I was touched, but I could not cover my emotion.

This singer seemed deeply consecrated. It is true that he did not have a wonderful voice, but the Christlike way in which he sang made the message of the song impressive. After the singing another young man preached a most convincing sermon on "The Sure Word of God." Every word was food for my hungry soul. Never before had song, sermon, and prayer taken such hold of my heart.

After the benediction, all three of the ministers hurried to the entrance to greet the people with a hearty handshake and a cheerful, "We are glad you came out tonight. We hope you will come again."

Not much was said on the way home; but there was no laughter and talking as there had been on the way to town. Everyone seemed to be meditating. A great lump remained in my throat. On our arrival at home we all hurried to bed. It was past ten o'clock, but I could not sleep. I longed to go someplace where I could pour out the burden of my heart. I wanted to tell Jesus I was sorry I had grieved Him by drifting into worldliness and sin.

When all the others were asleep, I got up quietly and went out among the trees. There in the darkness I knelt down. I did not know how to pray; I just knelt there and cried and hid my face from the stars that shone above me. My heart was so full that I wanted to say much. But my prayer was short like that of the publican, "God be merciful to me a sinner."

# 6

## The Preacher Explains the "Soul"

The next morning each of us got busy at the work father assigned us. I was to help him clean the fruit orchard. Haying was over, and harvest was coming on in two days. In those two days there was much to be done. Henry and Leonhard were getting the binders ready. Sister Mary went through the garden once more to see that all the weeds were out. When harvesting began, everyone would be busy in the field except mother and the little ones.

Father and I worked hard in the orchard until nine-thirty, when little brother Willie brought us a lunch. We sat down and rested while we ate. During these few minutes we talked about the experience of the previous evening at the tent. Among other things father said, "The people did not tell the truth about these folks. The ministers surely did not consider themselves too holy last evening to shake hands with the people, and their meeting was very good from the first song to the benediction."

Looking at me, he said, "Would you like to go again, Helen?"

"Oh yes!" I answered eagerly.

At noon, when every member was seated at the long family

table, father said, "If you all work hard and get your work done on time, we will attend another meeting tonight."

We were all happy about this; so, instead of resting awhile after dinner, most of us went to work immediately. When suppertime came, each assigned task had been completed. The supper dishes were washed in a hurry and soon all were ready to leave for the tent. This time we went in the wagon, so that more of the family could go.

We arrived at the tent in time to hear some of the song service that preceded the regular meeting. As I watched these people sing, I admired them for the work that they were doing. Their life of service was a blessing. As I thought of how I was wasting my life, my heart was filled with remorse that I had not appreciated my Saviour's love more.

The theme of the sermon that evening was, "The Soul." This greatly interested me, for well did I recall the humiliating experience I had had at confirmation school when I asked the minister to explain the subject to me. I also remembered that father told me I would understand about the soul when I was older. I felt that the time had now come. By the time the young minister finished his sermon it had all been made clear to me. It was indeed a great satisfaction to have the matter so wonderfully presented from God's Word.

I kept watching my father and mother to see if they were enjoying the sermon. They were eagerly taking in every word. I was glad, for I wanted them to enjoy it so much that they would wish to come back the next evening.

It was a lovely moonlight night, and we enjoyed the home-ward drive. When we were out of town a little way, father said, "This surely was another outstanding sermon. I must admit I never was clear on that soul question before. The topic for tomorrow night also sounds interesting. I guess we will start planning now to return."

Nothing could have pleased us more, for we greatly enjoyed those good songs and sermons. We were so encouraged by them that we did not grow weary from the heavy work during the day.

The next evening just as we were ready to start for town, George arrived to spend the evening. For a moment I was worried. I did not want to miss the meeting, and I feared he would not wish to go along to a meeting in a tent. After all, he belonged to the finest church in town. Father saw that I was puzzled, so he called to George, "We are all going to town to hear the new young preachers. Won't you come with us?"

George cheerfully answered, "All right, and I'll be glad to take some of your load." Mother and I got into his new carriage and were soon on our way.

I was very glad he was going to attend what I knew promised to be a good meeting. His talk about dances and other worldly pleasures did not interest me as it had only a few days before. I wanted much more to talk about what we had heard the previous evenings; but, knowing he had not attended any of the meetings, I thought it better to be quiet until I should see how he would enjoy this one. When we arrived at the tent, George said he would not go in for fear some of his church folks would see him and ridicule him. Mother and I went in with the rest of our family while he remained standing outside. At the close of the meeting the announcement was made that "The Image of Daniel 2" would be the topic for the next meeting. The image was shown on a large chart. Of course, we were interested and planned to return.

Harvesting had begun, but we stopped work early enough to go to the tent. Indeed, for weeks we did not miss an evening service.

# 7

## Father Quits the Meetings

After we had been attending the meetings in the tent for about three weeks, father began to disagree with some of the points presented by the young ministers. He said he did not care to go anymore. However, he did attend until one evening several of his friends called him out of the meeting and said to him earnestly and as if anxious for his welfare, "Sir, you are doing a great wrong by bringing your family to these meetings. These people are Seventh-day Adventists. Soon they will be asking you to keep Saturday as the Sabbath. Then you will have to become Jews. You are too sensible a man to take up with such a queer belief as that."

Father was very quiet on the way home that night. He did not sing with us as he had been doing other evenings; instead, we could hear him sigh occasionally. He knew if we continued to attend the meetings, everyone in the vicinity would soon despise us. The next evening he did not attend. However, he allowed us to go.

The following day as father and I were shocking bundles together behind two binders, he asked me questions about the last meeting. I was glad to tell him what I could remember.

27

"The good folk at the tent asked if you were ill, and sent their regards," I told him. Father only sighed.

Later he said, "You know, Helen, these people have the same ideas as the man who sold us that big book years ago. They are the people the Scriptures describe as wolves in sheep's clothing. They trample God's holy day underfoot and keep the old Jewish Sabbath. I think we had better quit attending their meetings."

"I don't think father will let us attend any more meetings," I told my brothers and sisters while father was napping after dinner. All of us were worried about it. We feared that he would ask us to work too late to get to the meeting.

Who dared ask him to let us attend again that night? My eldest brother finally said, "You will work again with father this afternoon. You ask him by four o'clock so we shall know in time what he says." Just then we heard father whistle. Then came the call, "All aboard!" Everyone hurried to his task, and the work moved on smoothly.

A little past three o'clock the dogs began to bark. As we looked, we saw two men coming from the railroad toward the house. Thinking they might be tramps, father said to me, "You had better run home and stay with mother until those fellows leave." We were working only a short distance from home, so I hurried to reach the yard before the men arrived. As they came up the hill, I noticed that the dogs were acting as though these men were friends. They wagged their tails and tried to jump up and play with their hands. The men were talking kindly to them.

As they came closer, I saw that they were two of the young ministers from the tent. They waved a friendly hello as they entered the yard. I was indeed happy, for I thought surely they would invite father to the meeting and thus help me out. They visited with mother while I hurried to the well for a pail of cold water. They were weary and thirsty from the three-mile walk in the hot sun. After a few moments' rest and a cold drink, they said they wanted to go to the field to see father.

28

As we left the door, mother handed me a jug of cold milk, some bread and butter, and some crisp young radishes and onions for our four-o'clock lunch.

On the way I asked, "Is it true that you break Sunday and keep Saturday as a rest day?"

Smilingly they answered, "We have not preached anything about Sunday or Saturday observance, so why do you ask us this question? We do not break Sunday; we leave it just as it is—the first day of the week. It has its purpose to fill in the weekly cycle the same as any other day; but we do rest on the seventh day, and that is Saturday. We keep it because God tells us in His Word that the seventh day is the Sabbath of the Lord our God. Does that answer your question?"

"We keep Sunday because Jesus arose on that day," I told him.

"Do you know what the Bible says about Sunday observance?" one of them asked me. But by this time we were nearing father, so I kept silent.

Father greeted the guests kindly, and they visited until the rest of the harvesters arrived. Then we all sat down and enjoyed the lunch together. After the men had hurried off toward town to get ready for the evening meeting, father joined me on our side of the field. He did not speak; and as I could see he was having a terrible battle, I did not say a word either. After quitting time we anxiously awaited word as to his plans for the evening, but he remained silent. After all the chores were attended to and supper was over, we were still waiting. Seeing our anxiety, father finally said, "You may go, but this will be your last evening at the tent."

We were hailed with the shouts of "Advents! Advents!" by some of our acquaintances on the street in front of the tent.

As we entered, the opening song was being sung. It seemed to me that the singers' hearts were heavy, for there was a note of sadness in their voices as they sang, "I would be, dear Saviour, wholly Thine."

That deep longing in my heart to be a Christian was stirred

anew by the words of this song. Everyone on the rostrum knelt while one of the ministers prayed a most earnest prayer. Tears rolled down his cheeks as he sought God to touch the hearts of the people in the vicinity. Our hearts were touched by this earnest prayer and by the wonderful sermon that followed. I was fully convinced at this meeeting that these people were sent from God. They were not false prophets and deceivers, but were preaching the message for our time. At the close of the meeting, as we stepped out of the tent, we saw people standing around making evil remarks about these "holy Sabbath keepers," as they called them.

"Are you going to continue to attend these meetings?" they asked me in none too kind a tone.

"I hope with all my heart that I shall not have to miss a single one," I replied.

While I was speaking, one of the leading men of the town and his wife stepped up and said, "You folks are foolish to attend these meetings! If you would stay away, these fellows would soon pack up and leave; and, if they didn't, we would see to it that their tent would be burned to the ground."

Aroused to indignation, I answered, "Very well, if this tent is burned down, I shall give your names as the suspects."

In the tent mother was talking to the ministers. "We are grieved that your husband has been influenced against us and our work," they were telling her. We said Good-bye to them with heavy hearts, for we were sure our attendance would have to stop.

# 8

# The Tent Attacked

A number of days passed in which none of us got back to town. We could not quite understand why we should not be permitted to attend those good meetings; but father said we could not go, and we had been taught to obey.

Friday noon we again saw two men coming from the railroad tracks toward our home. As they came closer, we saw that they were our Christian friends from the tent.

"Well, why have you come this time?" father inquired.

"We have come to help you finish the harvesting job so that you can come to the meetings again," they cheerfully responded.

"Since you men have come to help, I think I shall stay home and work on the threshing machine, for threshing is to begin soon," said my father.

So the ministers and the rest of us went to work on the last field of grain. We worked hard, and yet these servants of God talked to us about our souls' salvation. By four o'clock in the afternoon we had finished. Before we started home, they asked, "Wouldn't you like to kneel down and pray for your father that he might come to the meetings again and bring all of you as he used to?" This was a new experience for us, for never before had anyone come and asked to pray with us. After prayer we started home.

Father was surprised that we had finished so early, and he smiled as he saw the perspiration on the faces of these young ministers. They took a drink of water, then turned to start back to town. But father said, "You have worked hard this afternoon; now stay and have supper with us. After supper I will take you to town. I have to get some repairs for the machine; so I can do two errands in one."

"Thank you, sir," one of them said. "Maybe you can all come to the meeting this evening, since you got through early. Then you will do three errands in one."

Father smiled. "Well, maybe we can do that."

"Heaven, the Home of the Saved" was the topic for the evening. It was a wonderful message, indeed; yet all during the service we could hear the prejudiced people outside the tent. Some were furious because we had again come to the meeting. At the close they tried to frighten us by their threats. When we refused to be frightened, they said, "Very well, then, we shall resort to some other method to stop these meetings."

We told the ministers about the threats that had been made, but they did not seem much concerned. They said they had heard of such things before. As we walked away from the tent, we looked back. There those ministers stood alone, but it was evident that the peace of heaven rested upon them even when all the world seemed against them.

I feared those angry people would carry out their threats during the night; so on the way home I asked father if he thought they would bring harm to the young ministers. Father replied, "Why, no. These people around here are all Christians; they all belong to some church. All they are trying to do is drive these young fellows out of town. They would not dare to do anything to harm them."

Right behind the large tent was a small one in which two of the ministers slept. They were very tired that evening from the three-mile walk and their hard work in the harvest field, and they soon were sound asleep. The streets were quiet, and all the lights were out; but evil was at work in the hearts of a group of men in a secluded room a little way down the street. Among them were church leaders who should have been guiding wicked minds into right channels. Instead, they were working with Satan in an effort to hinder God's work in that place.

"What are we going to do with these deceivers? Are we going to let them sit here in these tents much longer? They are false prophets, and they are here for no good purpose! We must take steps at once to get rid of them." These were the remarks of one church leader.

Another one said, "These fellows are too lazy to work! They take great delight in sitting around on their holy Sabbath day, as they call it, pretending they are holy. I don't think we should tolerate them any longer on our streets."

A third church leader spoke up eagerly, "Tomorrow is these fellows' Sabbath, and they say they will not work on that day. Let's take all the seats from the tent and set them in the middle of the main street, leaving about fifteen or twenty feet beween them; in that way the last seat will reach clear down to the other end of the street. Let's remove their organ from the tent, and hide it. Then we'll watch those lazy devils run in the morning to get their seats off the street; and, when they cannot find their organ, they'll forget all about its being their holy Sabbath. If they find the organ, they'll be glad to carry it back, all right. That will give them plenty of work for one day."

"A good plan, boys!" said one of the older men. "That's a fine one! We shall have some fun with those young so-called preachers."

Four young men were selected to do the mischief. However, the four balked, saying they would not do the job unless they were paid for it. The other men at last agreed to give them $75. This was satisfactory, so the work began in earnest.

It was now a little past two o'clock. The organ, which had

33

been rented from the furniture store, was carried down the street, hoisted up to the roof of a store, and left there. The seats were carried out on the street. After this was accomplished, the men hurried back to carry away the pulpit. As they were taking it from the rostrum, one man stumbled. The noise awoke the ministers in the small tent in the rear, and they jumped out of bed to investigate.

The four marauders heard them coming, so they ran and hid between the buildings. When the ministers saw what had been done, they decided they had better call the marshal; but before this could be done, the four men dashed out from between the buildings and struck the younger minister on the head so hard that he fell. Then they began to kick him. The other minister called for help. This awakened the people, and in a moment lights could be seen all around. The ruffians, of course, ran and hid. The town marshal soon arrived and was told what had happened. He went to get the mayor of the town to help locate the troublemakers.

The marshal and the mayor were both good men, who knew how to handle the affair in a tactful way. They went back and told the young ministers not to touch the things on the street or the things that were disturbed in the tent. They assured them that everything would be put back in place by the ones who had done the damage, if they could be found. Then they hurried out into the dark, and before daybreak they had found the four young men. The mayor and the marshal stayed right with them until morning; then they took them down to the tent. There they made them put the rug back on the rostrum and replace the pulpit. The seats were carried back one by one and placed in order. Next they made the young men get the truck, go up on the roof of the store, get the organ down, and haul it back to the tent. It was scratched up so badly that they had to buy it from the owner of the furniture store and give it to the preachers.

By this time the streets were filled with curious people, and the young men who had wrought the damage felt much humiliated about the affair. They decided not to bear the reproach alone; so they gave the names of the church leaders and of others who had paid them to do the mischief. This caused a great disturbance in the town.

It was plain to be seen that God was on the side of these His servants; for everything was put in place, and they now owned the lovely eight-octave organ that they were only able to rent before.

Father was provoked when he heard who was involved in the planning of this wicked piece of work. "Those fellows claim to be good Christians," he said; "now we see what they are! They are just like the Pharisees in Christ's day. They lie in secret and plan to kill. I have no use for such church members!"

Mother said, "Let's quit early tonight so we can go to the meeting. Those young preachers need our encouragement. Maybe we can help them."

Mother's suggestion worked out perfectly, and a quarter to eight found us seated in the tent. It was well filled that evening, and many stood around the outside. Some came out of sympathy; others were curious to hear what would be said about the experience of the night before. The minister who had received the bodily injury was leading out in the song service as he had done other evenings. I shall never forget the opening song:

> I am a stranger here, within a foreign land;
> My home is far away upon a golden strand;
> Ambassador to be of realms beyond the sea,
> I'm here on business for my King.
>
> This is the message that I bring,
> A message angels fain would sing:
> "Oh, be ye reconciled,"
> Thus saith my Lord and King,
> "Oh, be ye reconciled to God."

Then the other minister offered a wonderful prayer. He invoked God's blessing to rest upon the inhabitants of the town.

His voice was filled with tenderness and forgiveness. It seemed that every word struck home to the hearts of the audience. After prayer this solo was sung:

> I have a Saviour, He's pleading in glory,
>     A dear, loving Saviour, though earth friends be few;
> And now He is watching in tenderness o'er me,
>     And O that my Saviour were your Saviour too.
>
> I have a Father; to me He has given
>     A hope for eternity, blessed and true;
> And soon He will call me to meet Him in heaven,
>     But O that He d let me bring you with me, too!
>
> For you I am praying, for you I am praying,
> For you I am praying, I'm praying for you.

There was no moving about, and even the whisperers on the outside were hushed as he sang. I was touched as I listened to those words, and again I said, "Lord, I want to be a Christian."

A most stirring sermon on the judgment followed. Not a word was said about the experience of the night before, but the hearers got the lesson; for, by the time the meeting closed, all those that stood outside had quietly slipped away.

# 9

## The Visit in the Field

The ministers of the town were still determined to keep their members from hearing any more truth; so they visited every member who had attended the tent meetings and made it plain to them that they were expected to stay away.

After they had checked up on almost all the other people in town, they came out to our house to labor with my father. Father argued with them and told them that their church leaders and members were a discredit to Christianity because of what had happened at the tent a few nights before. They shielded themselves, however, saying, "These young fellows have caused so much unrest and have agitated the people so with their sermons that the people are beside themselves." Then they went on to say that if these fellows stayed much longer, they would break up the peace both in the churches and in families. They begged father to cooperate with them to keep peace in the town.

As they were about to leave, father said, "Well, we shall never join their church; so we will stay away if that will help matters any." They bowed gracefully and almost kissed father's hands as they thanked him for his help in getting the young preachers silenced. So we were forbidden to go to the tent again.

One afternoon we were threshing near town. Sister and I were talking of how we longed to attend another meeting and of what a help these young ministers had been in changing our lives. While we were thus talking, sister looked up and said, "Look! There are three men coming toward us."

Two of them were the ministers from the tent, and the third was a friend of theirs, a visiting minister.

Stepping up to the threshing machine, they said to father, "We believe we need some more exercise, so we have come out to help pitch bundles." Not wanting to refuse them, father said the strongest one could help pitch bundles on my wagon, as I was very nearly tired out.

"The others may take their choice at any wagon," said father.

The strongest of the three men was the visiting minister, a stranger to me. Because the tent preachers had told him that my sister and I had enjoyed the sermons that had been preached, they had decided to walk out to see us.

The man assigned to my wagon worked hard pitching bundles, all the while talking to me about the message in which he knew I was interested. He seemed consecrated and Christlike. He was a perfect stranger to me; but what a blessing his visit proved to be! As he made plain to me God's love for sinners, my heart was filled anew with a deep desire to follow my Saviour all the way. I told him that I wanted to live the truth I had heard, but the way seemed too dark. I did not see how I could go ahead. He said, "God will open the way and lead you on if you will fully trust Him. Can you not launch out in faith even if you cannot see the way, and say, 'Lord, I will follow'?" I was silent and feared to make the vow, lest I should not be able to keep it. He saw I was weighing the question seriously; so, to help me in my perplexity, he said, "Let us bow our heads right here by this wagon, and talk to Jesus about it." We did, and he prayed a most earnest prayer, which was a source of real strength to me.

At five o'clock the three ministers were ready to return to town to attend to their duties. After they said Good-bye to father and the others at the machine, they came by where I was working. They spoke a few more words of courage and assured me they would all pray for me. Nothing could have brought more joy to me than their friendly visit. I told them we were forbidden to attend any more meetings, but I would try to visit them the following Sunday if I was permitted to go to town.

The visiting minister said, "Good-bye, my young sister. I may never see you again; so I ask you in the name of God to press forward and step over the line; there is only a step between you and your Saviour." He then quoted the words of a well-known hymn, adapting the chorus to fit my case.

> Oh, tender and sweet was the Father's voice,
>     As He lovingly called to me,
> "Come over the line, it is only a step,
>     I'm waiting, My child, for thee."

> "Over the line," hear the sweet refrain;
>     Angels are chanting the heavenly strain;
> "Over the line,"—why should you remain
>     With a step between you and Jesus?

Then they hastened away. As I thought of the momentous step that was before me, I again saw my weaknesses. I began to say in the words of the song—

> "But my flesh is so feeble," with tears I said,
>     "And the pathway I cannot see;
> I fear if I try I may sadly fail,
>     And thus dishonor Thee."

# 10

# My Sunday Visit

All the ministers of the town had decided to have a union service on Sunday morning to expose Adventism, and the services were to be conducted in the largest church. They secured an out-of-town speaker who claimed he knew the Adventists thoroughly. Father received a number of urgent invitations to attend and to bring the "misled" members of his family to hear this speaker and his exposure of the despised sect.

Sunday morning father said he was going to attend that big meeting, and a number of us could go along. I asked mother if I could go; I wanted to stay in town after the meeting to visit a girl friend part of the afternoon and, later, the people at the tent. The minister's wife had been friendly.

"You have worked hard all summer, Helen, and have not had a day off; I think you may stay in town," mother told me.

From every direction we could see the neighbors driving toward town to attend the big meeting. We were among the last ones to be seated. The service opened in a dignified, solemn way; but when the visiting speaker warmed up to his subject, all solemnity seemed to fade. His speech was harsh, critical, and caustic. He gave no proof from the Bible for his opinions.

40

After he finished, two of the ministers from the town spoke in the same vein. Each thrust only drove the truths I had heard deeper into my heart. I was more convinced than ever that the Adventists were right.

At the close of the meeting I saw my girl friend standing on the sidewalk. I hurried over to her and took hold of her hand, saying, "Hello, Emma!"

She turned quickly and jerked her hand away. Looking scornfully at me, she said, "You old Advent! You are no longer a friend of mine! I have heard how much you like those Jews at the tent. I am ashamed of you!" A number of other young people joined her, and before I could turn away, I was encircled by mockers.

I got away from them as soon as I could and began to look for my parents, but they had already started for home. My heart ached at the unkind treatment I had received from those who had been my friends. I did not know where to go now, for I could not go to Emma's house as I had planned. Because I did not want anyone to see the tears that were falling, I went to the depot and sat down in the waiting room.

At two o'clock some people from town came to the depot to bid Good-bye to some of their friends who had come to attend the union service. The train was due at two-thirty. They talked freely about the sermon. One of the women knew me quite well, so, when she noticed me, she came over and said, "I was glad to see you at church. Wasn't that a wonderful sermon this morning? After this, no one in this community should be deceived by those fake preachers." Then she went on telling some of the strange things she had heard elsewhere about the young ministers.

Finally I said, "I do not believe those tales! I have found these people to be good, honest, faithful Christians."

Just then, to my surprise, two ministers entered. Hurrying over to them, my friend cried out, "Helen is still upholding those Adventists after all that was said in the service this morning!"

Both the ministers looked at me scornfully. I knew that was no place for me, so I started for the door. Whereupon the minister who knew me best followed me outside, and called, "I want to talk to you, young lady."

I stopped, and this was his message: "Now, listen! We do not want to see you at that tent again. All the rest are staying away, and we expect you to stay away, too. Do you get it?"

Then he went back to join his crowd.

His words did not make much impression on me, for I left him and went straight to the tent. I had not had any dinner; but I had waited until I thought the people at the tent would be through with theirs.

At the tent I found no one. What should I do now? Finally I picked up courage to find the house where one of the ministers and his wife lived. To my great astonishment and joy I found all three ministers and their families together there. They gave me a warm welcome, and we had a pleasant afternoon together. Somehow I felt condemned in their presence with my rings and necklace on; so I took them off when they were not looking, and slipped them into my purse. At that time I had no knowledge of what the Scriptures teach about the wearing of jewelry, but I was impressed that it was wrong to wear it, despite the fact that not a word had been said to me by these friends on this subject.

I asked them many questions during the afternoon, and they answered from Scripture. The evening was drawing near, and I looked forward to the tent meeting. The song service lasted for some time, but no one came. I was the only listener. After a while, mother, Katie, and Leonhard came. They said father was attending some council meeting, so they came to hear the sermon. Mother knew she would find me there.

The study for the evening went straight to my heart. "The Handwriting on the Wall" was the topic. I fully resolved that night to take my stand for God's truth. I did not want to hear the words from Jesus, "Thou art weighed in the balances, and art found wanting." Daniel 5:27. Neither did I wish to be classed with those described in an inscription in an old German cathedral, which the minister quoted:

> Thus speaketh Christ, our Lord, to us:
> "Ye call Me Master, and obey Me not;
> Ye call Me Light, and see Me not;
> Ye call Me Way, and ye walk Me not;
> Ye call Me Life, and desire Me not;
> Ye call Me Wise, and ask Me not;
> Ye call Me Eternal, and seek Me not;
> Ye call Me Rich, and ask Me not;
> Ye call Me Just, and fear Me not;
> If I condemn you, blame Me not."

The next week the tent was taken down. I felt sad when I saw these witnesses for God and His truth leaving. The summer was gone, and I was not saved; but the Holy Spirit kept on speaking to me, and I kept saying—

> I can hear my Saviour calling,
> In the tenderest accents calling;
> On my ear these words are falling,—
>   "Come and follow, daily follow Me."

# 11

## *George and I at the Crossroads*

After the tent was taken down the first part of September, the one minister and his assistant who remained rented a small hall and announced that the meetings would continue three nights a week. A few persons who were not intimidated by the opposing ministers attended. However, none of our family returned to town for some time. We knew better than to ask father to let us go.

All during this period I kept praying God somehow would open the way so I could live the message that had come to my heart. Ministers, relatives, and friends kept coming to our house on Sundays to visit, and they seemed to insist on talking about the ministers who had been in town with the tent. They called them "twisters of the Scriptures." This grieved me, for I saw they were sowing evil seed. My poor father, who had already closed his heart to a large degree, seemed to believe many of their stories.

One week father was called away on some business, so Katie and I went to one of the meetings. The topics under consideration that night were "Daniel in the Lions' Den" and "The Three Hebrews in the Fiery Furnace." This message was indeed timely, for it greatly encouraged me to learn of God's wonderful care over His children if they will but fully trust Him.

As we approached the yard on our return home, we saw a team of horses tied to the hitching post near the house. George had brought his two brothers and a girl cousin to spend the evening. Henry and Mary were entertaining them.

We played a few games and popped some corn. When the corn and apples were ready to serve, the boys chose their partners. George chose me to be his partner.

For some time we talked about things that were of common interest to all in the room. George did not have much to say. Finally he asked me, "Where were you and Katie the forepart of the evening?"

"At a meeting," I told him.

George sighed deeply. I said nothing, and we munched away on our corn. Then in a rather sad tone of voice he said, "You are not the same as you used to be, Helen. Tell me what is wrong."

Try as I would, I could not keep back the tears, for I knew he did not understand the change that had taken place in my heart. Noticing how keenly I felt, he said softly, "Let's go for a walk so I can talk to you alone."

"It's past eleven, George," I said; "suppose you come back on Sunday."

"All right," he agreed.

George came the next Sunday, not to spend the afternoon as we had planned, but to take me to a neighborhood social. "We can talk over the things closest to our hearts as we drive along," he said.

"George," I replied, "I am sorry to disappoint you, but I cannot go with you."

He tied up his team, then turned to me and said, "We have been the best of friends, Helen, and you always seemed happy to enjoy anything that I planned for you. Now tell me what is the matter. Why can't you go along?"

"Because I want to be a Christian, and I have said Good-bye to all worldly amusements," I answered.

"Let's go for a walk," he said, taking my hand. It was a lovely, warm November afternoon, and we slowly walked down the road as we talked things over.

"You do not have to give up all the good times in life if you want to be a Christian," he said. "Look at me and some others of our crowd. We are church members. We belong to the best church in town, and we are enjoying these things. They are fun; there is nothing wrong in them. Come along. I just cannot go back to the crowd without you. You don't have to take part in the social if you do not care to, just so you are there. You will enjoy yourself again after you once get in the swing of things. Come, say you will go." Then he waited for an answer.

Many voices whispered, "Go." I almost weakened, for I did not want to hurt him. I stopped walking, and, turning to him, I said, "Let's make a bargain, George. You stay here this afternoon, and after supper let us two go to town and take in a meeting. I shall be glad to go there with you."

He turned and said, "I shall be glad to take you to town, but not to those meetings—never!" Just then he seemed to notice that I was not wearing the ring he had given me. "Where is your ring?" he asked.

"Home, in my jewelry box," I answered. He looked puzzled.

We started back toward the house. George was quiet. I knew he was disappointed. How happy I would have been if his desires had been the same as mine! But he seemed to resent even the thought of those good meetings. As we were nearing his carriage, he said, "I am sorry we can't agree, Helen. May I ask you once more to give up those religious notions and be yourself again and go with me?"

The conflict began to get stronger within. Voices kept saying, "Don't disappoint him; he is a fine young man as the world goes. You may never be able to live the message you have heard, anyway. It will be much easier to go with George than to press forward on the road you have chosen."

George stood with bowed head and with one foot on the hub of the buggy wheel, waiting for my answer.

I turned my back to him for a minute, for I did not know what to do. I looked to the sky and said silently, "Lord, I want to be a Christian. Help me make the right choice." A lump was in my throat, and the tears came. I swallowed hard, fighting them back; then I turned, and said, "I am sorry, but I cannot go, George."

Slowly he untied his team. Before he got into his carriage, he said in a low voice, "Shall we have to say Good-bye forever?"

"I hope not," I replied.

He stood a moment longer, hoping I would change my mind. When he saw that no other answer came, he got into his carriage. "I expect to see the ring on your finger when I come to see you again," he said, and then drove away.

I went to my room, where I lay on my bed and cried for a while before that awful tight feeling left my throat. I was glad when mother called and said it was time to do chores. I told mother after I came downstairs that I had gone through a terrible battle. I said that I did not want to hurt George, but I wished to be a true Christian. Consequently I had refused to go to the dance with him, and he had gone away hurt. I was sure he would never come back again.

Mother said, "Don't worry, dear. He will get over it. I think you made the right choice."

I felt that I had, too, even at the sacrifice of a dear friend. I felt that Jesus was pleased with my decision.

I never saw George after that, neither did his ring ever again decorate my hand. I prayed much for his conversion, but George remained with his church.

# 12

## At the Blacksmith Shop

After supper Katie and I asked mother to let us go to the meeting in the hall that night. She consented, so with joyful footsteps we walked the three miles to town.

The topic for the evening was, "The Importance of Obedience." The speaker closed with this remark: "Those who are not willing to consecrate their whole lives to God will be left outside." Then the beautiful hymn was sung:

> O weary soul, the gate is near,
>     In sin why still abide?
> Both peace and rest are waiting here,
>     And you are just outside.
>
> Forgiveness Jesus will impart,
>     To save your soul He died;
> How can you still offend His heart
>     By staying just outside?
>
> The day of life is passing by;
>     Soon night your soul will hide;
> And then "Too late" will be your cry,
>     If you are just outside!

A call was made at the close of this song for those to rise who wanted to take their stand for God. I longed to rise, but I trembled so badly that I could not force myself to stand. At the close of the meeting as the ministers shook hands with the people when they went out, Katie and I stepped back and waited so that we would be the last ones. I wanted to tell them that I meant to take my stand; but, before I could speak, they said, "Well, girls, when will you decide fully for God?" At this I broke down and cried, and could not answer them. My sister was silent, too. They assured us of their prayers as they bade us a kind good-night. It seemed that I found no relief for the burden that pressed on my heart. I searched for words to express my feelings, but I could not find them.

Father returned home on Tuesday; so the work went on in the regular way again. I lost all desire for food, neither could I sleep well. My parents noticed that something was wrong, and mother asked me on Friday if I was sick. I told her I was not, but that I wanted so much to be a true Christian and to live the message I had heard at the tent that I had no desire for food. Mother said, "You had better stop worrying about that, Helen; then you will be all right." All day Friday I kept talking to God, asking Him to give me strength to take my first step in keeping the Sabbath the next day.

On Sabbath morning after breakfast father assigned us our tasks before he went to his blacksmith shop to work. I waited a few moments and then followed him. I stood in the door for a while, but father acted as if he did not see me. I suppose he had an idea of what was on my heart, so he just ignored me; but I finally stepped up behind him and put my hand on his shoulder. He looked up at me rather surprised and said, "Why aren't you at work, Helen?"

I said, "Father, I want to be a Christian, and I feel I must obey God's commandments if I am to be a true follower of His."

Father turned pale as he said, "Child, what do you mean? Do you want to become a 'Jew'? Do you realize what a reproach you would bring upon us as a family?"

I started back to the door, blinded with tears. Father wept, too. We both stood in the door and wept for a moment. Then father said, "This will never do! You must forget these things. Come, I will go with you. We will get in the last of the corn from the field."

I felt defeated and also pained to think I had caused father to weep. I went with him, and we worked hard—but in silence.

Mother's parents lived in their own little house in our yard. At noon, when we came home, mother told us that grandmother was seriously ill. I loved my grandparents and felt sad about this news; so I went right over to see them. Grandmother was sick, indeed. She reached out and took my hand in her trembling feverish ones, saying, "Good-bye, dear; I am going to leave you. Be good and help grandpa so he will not get too lonely."

"Good-bye, dear grandma," I said. "We shall not be separated long, for Jesus will soon come. Then He will call you out of your resting-place and take you to heaven."

She opened her eyes wide and said, "Who told you that Jesus is coming soon?"

"The Bible says so, grandma," I said. "Shall I read it out of your Bible?" She looked surprised. Grandpa handed me their Bible; it was an old one, with both covers off, but I found the texts I had heard the minister read the night he spoke on the second coming of Christ. I had also read those same texts in that large book in the attic. I read 1 Thessalonians 4:13-18 and Matthew 24:30, 31.

"Oh, such a welcome message!" grandma said.

After dinner father and I went out and resumed our work.

Yes, grandma was really leaving us, for she could not speak when we came home in the evening. At three o'clock in the morning she passed away. Grandpa asked me to stay up with him the rest of the night.

The next day father sent word for a minister to come to take charge of the funeral. When the man arrived, he informed father that the minister father had sent for was away at a convention, and so he had come to take his place. As he had come before dinner and the funeral was not to take place until two-thirty, father and he had a good chance to visit before the other people gathered.

I went upstairs after dinner to help my younger brothers and sisters get ready for the funeral, and from the open stairway I could hear much of the conversation between father and the minister. I heard my name mentioned; so I listened. I did not get all the minister said at first, but I heard father say, "Yes, I am sorry I took my family to those meetings. My daughter Helen is very much affected by what she heard. Last Saturday she even wanted to keep the Jewish Sabbath."

The minister became excited about this and raised his voice as he said, "I think I shall have a good talk with her before I leave. I can see how she might be influenced by such ideas; she had some peculiar Bible questions about the soul and other things at the time she attended confirmation school, I have been told."

Needless to say, I did not care to talk to him, so I made my way from the house as quickly as possible. I took two of my little brothers by the hand and started for the buggy that stood in front of the blacksmith shop. We stood in the shop door and watched the neighbors coming from every direction. I was just going to put both little ones up on the buggy seat when I was startled by the nearness of the minister's voice as he said, "Oh, here I find you! I saw you coming over this way, so I left the folks. I want to talk to you.

"Your father tells me you are interested in the things you have heard at the Adventist meetings the past months. Am I rightly informed?" I told him he was. He then told me what he thought of young folks in their teens who thought they knew more about the Bible than their parents or ministers who had studied it all their lives. I listened to him. My little brothers pressed close to me. They did not understand why this man was talking to me as he did.

For a few moments I did not know whether I should answer him or not. I thought if he moved on, I would not speak, but he remained. Finally I replied, "I have never claimed that I knew more than my parents or the ministers, but I learned some Bible truths during the time the Seventh-day Adventist ministers held meetings. These have cleared up many puzzling questions in my mind."

Then he came up close to me and said, "And did they tell you what the soul is?"

"Yes, indeed," I answered. "They explained it perfectly, and all according to the Scriptures."

"Very well; tell me, then, what is a living soul?"

"You are a living soul, pastor," I told him.

"Well, what is your grandmother, who will be buried shortly?"

"She is a dead soul, according to the Scriptures. Genesis 2:7 says, 'The Lord God formed man of the dust of the ground, and breathed into his nostrils the breath of life; and man became a living soul.' "

He laughed out loud and said, "You are surely on the road to destruction! The soul is a holy thing, and cannot die; and no one can explain it."

Thinking he might carry a Bible in his pocket as the Adventist ministers did, I said, "If I could have your Bible, I could read to you some verses in which God speaks of souls dying when they sin. Ezekiel 18:4 and 20 speak plainly about it. So does Revelation 16:3."

"God forbid that I should let a sinner like you put your hands on my Bible!" he said, and he hastened away.

In his sermon during the funeral he tried his best to tell what the soul was. He tried to comfort the mourners by saying that grandmother was in heaven and was looking down on us. After the funeral he told our closest neighbor, a friend of his, to help father get that Adventist notion of Sabbath keeping out of me. This neighbor was a burly type of man, and I suppose the minister thought he could frighten me into giving up my convictions.

Grandpa heard the pastor make those remarks to our neighbor.

In the evening after we arrived home he said, "Helen, I have something to tell you. Will you please come over after supper and spend the evening with me?"

"Yes, grandpa, I'll be glad to," I replied.

During our visit we talked about the different things that had taken place during the day. All at once grandpa said, "Do you think your grandmother sees us and hears what we say?"

"No, grandpa," I said. "Ecclesiastes 9:5, 6, tells us that the dead do not know anything. Grandma will sleep in her grave until Jesus comes and awakens her." Then I read 1 Thessalonians 4:13-18 to him.

"The Bible is plain enough about that," grandpa said. "Well, Helen," he continued, "I overheard the minister today telling our neighbor across the way to help your father to get those Adventist notions out of your head."

"Good night, grandpa," was all I could answer.

# 13

## Conflict in the Orchard

We were nearing the close of another week. The question was still before me, "What shall I do? I do not want to break another Sabbath." I prayed as did David, "Unto Thee, O Lord, do I lift up my soul. O my God, I trust in Thee: let me not be ashamed, let not mine enemies triumph over me. Yea, let none that wait on Thee be ashamed: let them be ashamed which transgress without cause." Psalm 25:1-3. I was afraid that if I did not take my stand soon, God would pass me by, and I should be lost.

On Friday I said, "Mother, I am going to ask father once more to let me keep the Sabbath. I want you to help me."

Mother wept as she replied, "Oh, Helen, why do you want to run against a brick wall through which you can never go? Father will never let you keep the Sabbath."

"I want to be a whole Christian or none at all," I said. "I have given up all worldly pleasures; my whole desire now is to obey God fully."

I spent much of Friday night in prayer. I asked for wisdom and strength to go ahead in the right way. All too soon day began to break. I dreaded to go through the experience again of asking and being denied; but I must if I hoped to win. God will open the way, I reasoned with myself.

Soon I heard father call, "Time to get up!" We all hurried out and attended to our tasks. After breakfast father went to the orchard to cover the trunks of some of the young trees so that the rabbits could not eat off the bark during the winter. The rest all got busy doing their respective duties. I told mother how bad I felt about disobeying God longer. "I am going out to ask father once more," I said.

I started slowly toward him. He saw me coming, and this time he did not talk kindly to me. He turned quickly as I came near and asked, "Why aren't you at your work? I know what is on your mind. I will help you to forget it!" and he started toward me. He picked up the spade he had with him and threatened to use the broad side of it on me if I said one word about what he called the "nonsense in your mind."

I backed up against a tree and covered my face with my hands. I could not bear to look at father's angry face. He scolded, becoming loud and abusive. All at once I heard someone coming from behind me. I did not dare to look around for fear more trouble might be hanging over me. Just then father said, "Good morning, neighbor!"

My heart almost sank when I heard a voice respond, "Good morning. What is going on here?"

Father told him he was scolding his girl for wanting to keep the Jewish Sabbath. Father did not have to say more. This man, the one to whom the minister had spoken about me, seemed to feel he had the right to say anything he pleased. He pictured the Adventist people as the worst folk on earth and said many disrespectful things. It was hard to keep from speaking; but we were taught from early childhood to respect our elders and never to talk back. He kept on shouting and was so angry that he was beside himself. I was afraid he was going to harm me. "Why don't you talk?" he shouted.

I said in as calm a way as I knew how, "There are a number of things I should like to say, but I fear you will not listen."

"Speak on!" he shouted.

I then said, "I was talking to my father. The problem under discussion concerns only our family."

He became furious. He ran up to father and said, "Let me have her for just one week! I will get those wild ideas out of her. I will lock her in a dark room, give her dry bread and water once a day, and a hard whipping three times a day. That will cure her!"

Grandpa happened to step out of his house just then, and hearing the neighbor's shouting, he hastened to my rescue. I did not dare move away from the tree for fear the neighbor would seize me before help arrived. I was thankful when grandpa took me by the hand and led me to his house. He said, "I do not see why that minister wanted to set this madman on your trail."

I could not speak for some time; I just sat and cried. Grandpa tried to comfort me by saying, "You had better quit trying to be different from the way you were taught. Keep Sunday and live as your folks do. That will be much easier, and you will be saved, too. I am afraid if you say another word about keeping the law, your father will throw you out penniless. Where will you go then and what will you do if you get sick? You had better think it over and be content as you were before."

I said, "I know you mean well, grandpa, but if I want to be a true Christian, I cannot be content with the life I lived before I knew this truth. My eyes have been opened to God's requirements. If I want to be happy, I must advance and live what I know to be right. Let me have your Bible, grandpa. I want to read something to you. I hope I can find the texts that I want. Oh, here is one! Listen to it. 'Hereby do we know that we know Him, if we keep His commandments. He that saith, I know Him, and keepeth not His commandments, is a liar, and the truth is not in him. But whoso keepeth His word, in him verily is the love of God perfected: hereby know we that we are in Him. He that saith he abideth in Him ought himself also so to walk, even as He walked.' 1 John 2:3-6.

"Here is another good text: 'He that hath My commandments, and keepeth them, he it is that loveth Me: and he that
loveth Me shall be loved of My Father, and I will love him,
and will manifest Myself to him.' John 14:21. I know that God
will provide for me if I do His will. There is a text that says so.
It is in Luke, I think. No, here it is in Mark 10:29, 30: 'Jesus
answered and said, Verily I say unto you, There is no man
that hath left house, or brethren, or sisters, or father, or mother,
or wife, or children, or lands, for My sake, and the gospel's, but
he shall receive an hundredfold now in this time, houses, and
brethren, and sisters, and mothers, and children, and lands, with
persecutions; and in the world to come eternal life.' I believe
these promises."

Just then mother came to the door and called me. She said
father and the neighbor were coming to the house. She feared
what would happen if they found me not working. She handed
me a basket, saying, "Hurry to the shed and get me a basketful
of cobs and wood." I did so, and I also got some water from the
well. Then I went out to help Henry fix the fence around the
haystacks a little way from the stable. He was glad for my help.
Seeing that I felt distressed, he tried to talk about all sorts of
things to get my mind off my troubles. Tears kept coming, for
I felt terribly defeated to think that I was again breaking the
commandments.

The old neighbor sat on the porch and watched until nearly
noon; then he started home. As he passed us, he called to me,
"Remember, I will be back next Saturday morning to see that
you are at work."

# 14

## Sabbath in a Strawstack

The week following was one of darkness. I felt depressed and discouraged. It seemed that each week it grew harder to step forward. All week I prayed for God to come to my aid. I did not want to go back. To feel I was not victorious in fully living for Him was almost more than I could bear.

The weather was balmy. Father said Thursday evening, "I hope this Indian summer lasts a few days longer so we can get all the little odd jobs done before the cold winter sets in." The next morning he sent each of us to do our duties. My assignment was to finish a piece of plowing in a field about two miles from home. Father helped me hitch up the horses to the plow. He said he was going to town on some business, but he would stop on his way home to see how I was getting along.

I was glad to go away all by myself. Only old Fido, the family dog, went with me. I longed to get away where I could talk to God and no one could hear me. After I had my work well started, I stopped the horses behind a hill where I was sure no one would see me. I wanted to bring my burdens to Jesus before father returned from town; so I knelt down behind the plow and prayed most earnestly. I told the Lord how much

I wanted to follow Him fully and how I yearned to keep the Sabbath the next day. All at once I heard someone blow his nose. I got up quickly and looked around to see who was near. There stood father only a few feet away.

He evidently had heard my petition, for his eyes were filled with tears. He said nothing, but turned and walked back to his team, and started toward town. At noon I did not eat the lunch I had brought with me, for I was not hungry. After the horses had rested and finished their oats, I started my work again. Dark clouds began to come up in the northwest, and a bitterly cold wind blew strong. By about three-thirty it began to snow. I finished my field at four o'clock and got home before sundown. Father met me in the yard when I drove in and asked why I had come home so early. I told him I had finished the field. He was pleased, and as he saw I was cold, he said he would take care of the horses; so I went to the house. I was chilled through and was very tired. I went to bed as soon as the chores were done.

The burning desire to go forward in what I knew to be right and the dread and fear of what would happen again in the morning would not allow me to sleep. When Katie came to our room, I said to her, "Let's start together in the morning. It will be much easier, and maybe we shall win if we ask father together to let us keep God's commandments."

Katie said, "No! I am afraid. If you go ahead, you go alone." Then she went to bed and was soon sound asleep. It looked as if I had to go alone.

How much I wanted to put my arms around my father and mother and tell them I did not want to cause them any pain. I only wanted to obey my Lord and keep His commandments! However, I knew the minute I mentioned the commandments their hearts would be closed to me again. As I reasoned thus, I heard father wind the alarm clock, and soon everyone was sound asleep except me.

I prayed in silence for some time. It seemed my heart was so burdened it would burst, and I could not keep from crying.

I put my head under the covers and the pillow over my face, for I did not want anyone to know I was struggling in a dark valley. But in spite of all my muffling, Katie heard me. She began to admonish me, "You might as well give up your desires until you are older, Helen, for I see it is impossible to live now what we have heard. You had better stop worrying about it."

Brother Leonhard slept in the adjoining room and was awakened by our whispers, so he tiptoed in to see what was wrong. He said, "Helen, I want to be a Christian, too. But it is impossible to keep the Sabbath, so let's forget it for a while. Please don't say another word about the Sabbath. I know father will drive you away from home if you do. Where will you go then? You will not get any money, and everyone will hate you."

Yes, I knew all that. I loved my parents and my brothers and sisters and grandfather. How could I leave them? The more I thought about it, the bigger the lump became in my throat.

Katie said, "You had better go to sleep. Dismiss these things from your mind. Then all will be bright again."

Soon we heard someone come up the stairs. Sh! Sh! Katie drew the covers over her head. Leonhard quickly jumped into his bed. A match lighted the candle at the head of the stairs. Mother was there. She had heard our whispering and had come up quietly to see what was going on. She came straight to my bed. She thought I might be sick because I had gone to bed without supper. I said, "No, dear mother, I am not sick. I was only praying God to help me, for the way ahead seems so dark."

She put her hand on my head and said, "You are too young to take life so seriously, dear. Do you know that tomorrow is your birthday? You will be eighteen years old. I know the cross you want to take upon you is too heavy for your young shoulders. Cheer up! Quit thinking about it and go to sleep."

She blew out the candle and quietly went downstairs. Father was sound asleep.

When I was left alone again, I could plainly see that—

I must needs go home by the way of the cross,
    There's no other way but this:
I shall ne'er get sight of the gates of light,
    If the way of the cross I miss.

My decision was made. I had surrendered all. Now I had peace and I fell asleep. I rested well for some time. All at once I was awakened by a terrible fear. I was trembling from head to foot. I had dreamed that our rough neighbor had arrived and was choking me. He kept saying, "I will see to it that you will not keep Sabbath!" I trembled for some minutes, even when I knew it was only a dream. I thought, "Perhaps that is what he plans to do if he keeps his word and comes over in the morning." I prayed God to give me strength to bear with patience whatever the morning would bring.

The thought then came to me to get away early before the neighbor would arrive. Just then the alarm went off. It was still dark, and the night had passed swiftly. The wind was up and the snow was falling.

Soon father called, "Time to get up!" Everyone hurried from bed and got to work. After all were outside, I put on my coat, took my Bible and a copy of the *Review and Herald* under my arm, put my watch in my coat pocket, and went down to mother's bedroom. She was still in bed. I said, "Mother, I am going to keep Sabbath today. In order to avoid trouble, I am going to leave while it is dark. I am going where I can spend the Sabbath quietly. I shall be back after the Sabbath closes."

"Surely the evil one is leading you," mother said.

I said Good-bye, and went out into the dark, stormy night. I walked about a mile to one of our haystacks, thinking I could bury myself in it to keep warm. But no matter how hard I tried I could not dig into it. I knew there was a strawstack about half a mile from town, so I hurried toward it. I found it easy to make a roomy opening there. I made it large enough so I could sit in it comfortably. After I got inside, I worked the straw back into the opening so it was all closed up, leaving only a small hole to let in enough light so that I could see to read.

After I had rested a little while, it grew light enough so I could read my watch. I noticed that it was then only the hour when we usually got up. I could not figure out why father had got us out so early.

I could perhaps have gone to the home of the Adventist workers, who still lived in town, but I felt quite sure father would search for me during the day. If he found me at their house, it would cause them unnecessary grief. They did not know I was keeping Sabbath until later in the day.

I enjoyed the quiet hours in seclusion, and I felt the Lord was very near as I studied and had my devotions. Some cattle and sheep were eating from the strawstack. I enjoyed watching them.

This strawstack was only a short distance from the main road we always took to go to town. As I was reading, I heard a team going by. I peeped out to see if it might be father, and, sure enough, it was our team, but only grandpa and Katie were in the buggy. Father had sent them to the house of these workers to fetch me home if I was there. When told I was not there, they returned home. Father did not believe the story. He thought the minister and his wife were hiding me in their home, so he sent grandpa and Katie back again. He asked grandpa to search the house. These good folk were surprised to see grandpa and Katie back again. They said, "You may search the house if you do not believe us." Katie and grandpa knew these people would not lie to them, so they drove home again. I saw them go by each time. Knowing what it meant, I stayed quietly in my hiding place.

Since I knew there was to be a meeting that night in the hall, I stayed in seclusion until after darkness set in. Then I crawled out, shook the straw from my hair and clothes, and went to the service. There was no one at the hall when I arrived except the minister and his assistant. They were glad to see me. After talking a bit about the experience of the day, we had a season of prayer. As we arose from our knees, I heard someone enter. I did not dare to look to see who was coming for fear it might be father. I heard the footsteps coming up behind me, so I closed my eyes and took a deep breath to brace myself for what I feared would happen. The approaching person came and sat down right beside me. I then looked up and to my happy surprise it was my sister Katie. I clasped her hand in mine. We greatly enjoyed the short but comforting Bible study on "The Reward of the Overcomer."

After the benediction Katie said to me: "You'd better be prepared for the crisis." My friends looked at me and said, "We will pray for you. Be of good courage." On our way home Katie told me that the neighbor was on hand bright and early Sabbath morning and he was so angry when he saw he was defeated that he almost ran back home. I asked her, "Do you know why father got up so early this morning?"

She said, "He was surprised himself because it was dark so long. After looking at his watch, he said the hands must have got caught somehow when he set the alarm, with the result that it rang two hours early."

"Katie," I said, "I believe God's hand was in this to provide a way of escape from this harsh neighbor and the persecution I would have had to endure on Sabbath."

Mother and the younger children had retired when we arrived home. Father had been called to help a neighbor with a sick horse. Mother got up when she heard us come in, and she was glad to see me back. She told us to hurry to bed before father returned, so that nothing would happen that night. Father arrived soon after we retired, but he went to bed as soon as he found out I had returned.

Although weary, I could not sleep. After everyone else was sound asleep, I got up and lit the little bedroom lamp. I read in the Gospels about the sufferings of Christ. Thus my faith was strengthened.

# 15

# The Crisis

After reading about the sufferings of Christ I felt strengthened for whatever the morning might bring. I put my Bible
back in my coat pocket, then retired and soon fell asleep. I
slept soundly until father called, "Time to get up!" Everyone
hurried out to do his work. I met father as I was going to feed
the chickens and said, "Good morning, father," but he did not
answer. Nor did he speak a word until we were all seated
around the breakfast table and grace had been said.

I had begun to feel the need of some food. During those
trying hours I could not eat; but now a warm drink and the
soft-boiled eggs on the table, with some of mother's freshly
baked kuchen, made me hungry. I picked up my spoon,
ready to begin my breakfast. But even though I was so hungry,
I was not to have that pleasure.

Father commanded, "Put down that spoon, Helen! You shall
not eat a bite until you answer my questions."

I put down the spoon, and for a moment I thought I would
faint. It seemed I could not stand further strain. I buried my
face in my hands for a moment, and asked God for strength to
bear the coming moments and for wisdom to answer father's

questions correctly. Then I put my hands down. Sister Mary, who sat at my left, reached under the table and held my hands tightly. It seemed to help steady my nerves. Katie sat on my right and pressed tightly against me. No one ate. Everyone sat silent. I could see the tears coming to mother's eyes. The younger children began to cry, for they saw that father was angry.

"Where were you yesterday?" father demanded.

"At Meyer's strawstack," I answered.

"What were you doing there?"

"I kept the Sabbath."

"What! Kept the Sabbath? Now, tell me, Helen, will you give up those 'Jewish' ideas, or not?"

I could not answer. Again the question was put to me, but I could not speak.

In desperation father said, "Now I am going to ask the question once more. This time I demand an answer! I want to know if you will give up keeping the old 'Jewish' law?"

Through tears I looked into poor father's angry face and said, "Father, how can I give up what God asks of me? I have given up worldly pleasures, and I have given my life to God. Now I want to obey Him."

Father jumped up and came for me. I stood up, for I feared what was coming. He seized my hair with one hand and with the other he took hold of my right arm. In a moment he had me through the door out on the porch. He tore my right sleeve completely out, then he began to beat on my head with his fist. I felt no pain, but I soon fell unconscious. When I came to, I could hear mother and the rest of the family sobbing. But I could not move my body.

Grandpa, hearing the commotion, hurried out of his house. When he saw what was going on, he rushed over and wanted to help me. Mother and the rest did not dare to touch me, for father stood right over me. I heard grandpa say to father, "I am surprised at you! A man who professes to be a Christian to treat your child like that! I've heard of folks treating their dogs cruelly, but I have never seen a parent treat his child this way."

"You keep out of this!" father angrily commanded.

Grandpa stepped back, but father followed him and began to argue. Good old Fido began to lick my face. Upon feeling his warm tongue, I came to fully, got up, and headed for the barn. I felt the need of reaching a place where I could lie down. As soon as I had crawled up into the hayloft and lain down on the hay, all went blank.

Suddenly I heard my little brother, Reinhold, say, "Sister, you had better get away! Father said he would throw you down if he found you up here. He says you cannot stay here because you became a Jew." He was crying as he hurried away, for he feared father would whip him if he found him with me.

In a moment I heard father coming toward the barn, so I jumped down about ten feet from the south hayloft door. I ran to the creek, which flowed right past the southwest end of the barn, and crawled along under the weeds for a little way until I was out of sight. I started for a large dam we had about a quarter of a mile south of the farm. Fido seemed to understand that I was in serious trouble, for he kept close to my heels all the way. When I got behind the dam, I sat down and tried to think of all that had taken place.

I was cold, penniless, and homeless. I looked at the sun as it came up from behind the hills. It seemed to shine differently from the way it had before. "What shall I do now?" I asked myself. "My dress is torn. I have no coat, nor anything to put on my head to cover my tousled hair. Where shall I go?"

The sky was clear, but a cold northwest wind was blowing. As I walked far enough up the hill so I could get just a glimpse of home once more, I wept bitterly. For a time it seemed that I could not bear the thought of leaving all my loved ones. I might never see them again.

As I was thus battling with myself, I heard a little weeping voice. I looked up and listened. Fido, with his keen ears, heard the voice and started toward the creek. A moment later he came up the hill toward me, and behind followed my little brother,

Eugene. I ran over and took him in my arms, and we cried together for a while.

"I do not want to go back home!" he sobbed. "I want to go with you, Helen!"

Of course I could not take him along; neither could I keep old Fido. The only way I could get Eugene to go back home was to send him on an errand.

"Listen, Eugene," I pleaded, "I am cold. Will you go home and tell Katie I want my coat and cap? Fido will go with you."

Fido did not want to go, either; but I said, "Fido, you see Eugene home." He put his tail between his legs and started toward home with Eugene following him.

Father was standing by the well when brother entered the yard. The little fellow was so anxious to get the coat to me that he called out when he saw father, "Sister is cold! She wants her coat!"

"She cannot have anything from this place until she quits being a 'Jew,'" father growled and started for the house.

Katie happened to hear what was said, so she ran upstairs and quickly threw my coat and cap out of the back window. She feared father might lock the wardrobe. One of my little brothers was still standing behind the house crying about the happenings of the morning. Noticing him, Katie said, "Edward, take that coat and cap and run along the creek until you find Helen. Give them to her. Then hurry back the same way you went, so father won't see you."

She had just closed the window when father started up the stairs. He locked the wardrobe and went down again, not knowing that my coat and cap were on their way to me.

Taking the coat and cap from Edward, I kissed him Good-bye, then watched him disappear behind the weeds along the creek.

# 16

## Refuge

Where should I go now? What should I do?

These questions were uppermost in my mind as I walked along the creek bed the three miles to town. I arrived before the people were on their way to church. I was glad I didn't have to meet anyone, for I almost staggered. It seemed impossible for me to carry my weight.

"I had better look up the minister and his assistant," I thought, "and find out what they think I should do."

The minister opened the door when he saw me coming. He and his family cordially invited me in. They gave me a chair and I sat down for a moment, my head swimming.

When I took off my coat and cap and they saw my torn sleeve and my bruised forehead and tangled hair, they asked, "Whatever has happened to you, Helen?"

"Please, I would like to wash my face and comb my hair first," I choked, trying to suppress the tears.

"Of course you would, dear," said the minister's wife. "Come with me."

When I related to them the experiences of the morning, their hearts were touched. Yet they were happy to know that God had given me strength to go through these trials.

They soon got me something to eat, but even though I hadn't eaten for many hours, I seemed to have no appetite. I could hardly force myself to swallow. My throat and tongue were so dry that even water was repulsive.

After talking things over, all thought it best for me not to stay in town but to take the afternoon train north about twenty miles to a town near which the minister's parents lived. They feared that other trouble would come to me if I stayed where nearly everyone had hardened his heart against Bible truth. They gave me money for my fare, and the minister's wife accompanied me to the station. I purchased my ticket, and then we sat down in a corner and visited while waiting for the train to arrive.

All at once we were disturbed by the loud laughter and talking of some folk as they entered the door. They seemed to expect friends to arrive on the incoming train. When they saw me sitting and talking to the Adventist minister's wife, they began to make rude remarks. I acted as though I did not hear them. Finally two women, who had taken a bitter dislike to me ever since I began going to the tent meetings, stepped up to me. One of them said in a sarcastic tone, "You don't seem to see us anymore since you became friends with the Adventists. Maybe you have become holy, as they think they are."

I did not answer. The minister's wife put her hand on mine when she heard how sneeringly they all laughed.

Then the other one said, "Maybe she has begun to keep the holy Sabbath, too!" Again a chorus of loud laughter filled the waiting room.

It was nearly time for the train, so I got up. I thought it would be better if we stepped out on the platform and waited. As we started for the door, the first woman who had spoken took hold of my arm, saying, "Won't you tell us if you are keeping the Sabbath day or are you ashamed to tell?"

"No, indeed," I said. "I am not ashamed to tell you that I am keeping the day God commands us in the Scriptures to keep!"

"That is Sunday, is it not?" she said.

"No, it is the seventh day, the Sabbath of the Lord our God," I answered her.

She then roughly let go of me and said, "You fool!" and spit at me.

What a relief to hear the train pulling in! I took a seat on the west side of the coach so that I could take one more look at the dear old home as the train went by. How lonesome I was! How I longed for comfort! I took my Bible from my coat pocket. Upon opening it, I caught sight of this verse: "Thine ears shall hear a word behind thee, saying, This is the way, walk ye in it." Isaiah 30:21. I felt sure that the voice I had heard *was* leading me in the right way.

The minister had telephoned to his father, who lived about seven miles in the country, and asked him to meet the afternoon train. He and his youngest daughter, Emma, were at the depot when I arrived. It was just turning dusk when we reached the farm home, where a good warm supper was waiting for us.

During the night I dreamed I was in a deep dungeon. I wandered around in the dark trying to find my way out, but could not. I finally saw my lost condition and began to cry for help. When I looked up and saw how far it was to the top, I almost became discouraged. I tried to climb up on the steep sides, but always I fell back. I had been calling for help for some time when I looked up and saw a bright figure standing at the top looking down. I heard Him say, "I will help you if you will reach up and let Me take your hand." I at once reached up, and His strong hand pulled me to the top. I brushed the dirt from my clothes, then looked around to see where I should go. Two roads were before me. I asked, "Which one is the way to heaven?"

The One standing near showed me the road I was to take, but it was not cleared. In it I saw huge rocks and sharp thorns over which I had to climb. At the place where I entered it was quite wide. But, as I looked, I saw it grew more narrow all the way up, and there were obstacles to encounter all the way. At the end of the road shone a beautiful light. The One standing by me pointed to the light and said, "If you wish to enter there, you must be willing to go all the way."

In my dream the first obstacles seemed the largest. After I had gone some distance, I looked back to see where my loved ones were. I saw them slowly slipping downward on a smooth road that sparkled like glass. Some man was walking a little way ahead and was telling them that this was a much better road than the one I had chosen. I saw that some of them wanted to come and join me on the higher road, but they kept slipping, slipping. At the end of the sparkling road I could see a great chasm. I was in terrible distress and cried out, "I do not want them to slip clear down to that dark hole! I want to go after them and bring them up on this road!"

The One near me said, "Go!"

I hurried after them and turned them around one by one. When our faces were turned toward the upward way, we tried to go forward. But we could make no headway, for the road was so slippery. The man who had led them on stood laughing. He kept saying, "You will never make it!" I tried to push them so we would get a start but I was not strong enough to move them. In my terrible distress I began to cry to God for help. The answer came, "If you want to bring your loved ones with you, then you will have to get down on your knees," so I dropped to my knees. At once I got a start, and I called to the others to get on their knees also. When they did, we made good progress.

Some stayed far behind, but they kept on trying. I was glad all were trying to reach the higher road. Many dark figures were walking beside them and pointing the other way; but as long as they kept going on their knees, they were coming along all right. When I awoke from this dream, I was wet with perspiration. Truly the helping Hand had reached down to rescue me! Would the rest of the dream be fulfilled and my loved ones be led on toward God? And if so, would it be only some of them, or could it ever include them all, even father?

# 17

## Escape

"A business meeting of the church will be held next Wednesday evening," announced the minister the first Sabbath I attended church. "All the members are urged to be present." I learned before long that my case was to be considered. What should they do with me? Should they give me employment somewhere, or should they send me to school?

Some members felt that it would be wrong to send me away to school without my father's consent. They thought it might change his heart if two or three members would drive home with me and talk the matter over with him. "Perhaps he will even pay part of her expenses," some of them reasoned.

But the young minister from the tent meetings objected to this plan. "I know her father, and I am sure this plan would be a mistake," he said.

When they called me in and asked me what I thought, I agreed with him. "Father always means what he says; he told me not to enter the yard again until I had given up my religious ideas," I explained. I also told them that I was sure father would object to my going to school; and I was afraid if I got back home again, I should have to go through another dreadful experience.

Some still insisted that the plan be carried out; so they appointed four members to drive home with me the following day.

We arrived at my home about eleven o'clock. Father saw the carriage drive into the yard, so he stepped out on the porch to greet his visitors. My heart throbbed harder and harder as we approached the house. We stopped near the gate. Father acted rather surprised when he saw who the visitors were. I could not keep from crying when I came near him. I wanted to greet him heartily, but he would not even shake hands with me. This hurt me so much that I almost cried aloud. Mother met us at the door. We clasped each other tightly and wept for a time before either of us spoke a word. She finally said, "I am so glad you have come back, Helen!" I then left her and hurried through the house to see all my brothers and sisters before father came in. The few days I had been away seemed like a month.

When I saw Leonhard, I said, "I am sure I have experienced a real conversion now. I did not *see* anything, but peace filled my heart when I fully accepted Christ and began to serve Him."

"I wish I had taken my stand with you," Leonhard said, wiping his eyes. "It would be much nicer if I could be with you. Someday I will come and stand by you as I did during confirmation school."

The visitors, father, and all of us sat in the front room. Everyone sat and waited to see what would happen next. The two men talked about various things and tried to interest father, but he was reluctant to talk. When they saw they were not getting very far with their visit, they mentioned their mission. Father listened for a moment, then stood up and said angrily, "You get out of this house! You are to blame for the trouble that has come into our home! Now get out!"

Quickly leaving the house, they got into the buggy and seemed ready to drive away. I had to do or say something quickly. Tremblingly I stepped close to father and said, "Father, I had decided to go away to attend a Christian school; but these good folks brought me back to you to see if you will give your consent."

Father responded in a loud voice, "Your place is here at home, provided you fall in line and give up your Adventist notions!"

"I would be glad to stay home, father," I answered; "but I cannot give up this truth which has become dearer to me than life itself."

Chasing me, he cried out, "No! A thousand times no! You cannot stay here and be different from the rest of the family!"

Quickly I got into the carriage. As we drove away, we could hear father's frenzied voice, "I am going to put you in the reform school! You fellows stop and put her off! If you don't, I will send the marshal after you!"

After the church members had heard the report of our experience at home, they said, "What more do we want? Let us take up a collection and send the girl to Union College." It was agreed that I should go to this Adventist school in Nebraska, and the collection was taken.

Just as we were leaving the church, two men in a buggy drove up. One of the church members said to me, "I am sure that is the marshal. If he wants to see you, he will have to see you at our house." Soon we were over the hills.

The telephone was ringing as we entered the house. It was one of our friends calling. He said that the marshal and a relative of mine had arrived. "We told these men that Helen was staying at our home, but that she was spending the night with you folks. They want to talk with her; so will you bring her right over?"

"Yes, we will take Helen right over," he agreed.

There were two good roads leading to our friend's home. These men waited awhile, and when we did not arrive as soon as they thought we should, they decided they had better drive to where we were, as they feared I might get away. They took one road, and we were on the other; so we failed to meet.

74

When they arrived at the home we had just left, they were told that we had driven over to the friend's home whence the telephone call had come. In disgust they drove away.

Hearing the telephone ring and thinking that a neighbor who had been very sick might be trying to get a doctor, the woman took down the receiver and listened. She heard the marshal give someone at my hometown the following message: "We have tried to get her, but she seems to succeed in getting out of our way. We will not run after her any longer. We found out, however, that she is taking the early morning train and is leaving for some school in Nebraska. She will be through there about seven o'clock in the morning. Take her off the train there."

"Very well," was the reply on the other end of the line.

I almost collapsed when I heard that they were planning to take me off the train, for I feared the worst was yet before me. I pulled my chair close to the stove. I was cold and tired. My tongue seemed to cling to the roof of my mouth. Burying my face in my hands, I was almost asleep when I heard one of my friends say, "Well, it is past midnight. We must act quickly. What shall we do to keep this girl from having any trouble when the train arrives at her hometown?"

One of the men suggested that they hitch up the fastest team and take me two stations beyond my hometown and let me board the train there. This plan was agreed upon.

Seeing I was nearly worn-out and not accustomed to traveling alone, one of the men thought it would help me to have someone go with me. Turning to his daughter, he said, "You have wanted to go to Lincoln to visit your sisters; here is your chance. Can you be ready in fifteen minutes to make the trip with Helen?" She was overjoyed. She and her mother rushed to her room. In a few minutes the suitcase was packed. While the son got the team ready, her mother packed a lunch for us.

It was a cold, stormy night, and we were chilled through by

75

the time we reached the railway station. In fifteen minutes the train arrived. I did not relax, however, until we got past Sioux City. I felt sure that from there on I was not being followed. I was terrorized by father's statement that he would put me in reform school. In all the excitement none of us stopped to think that father did not have the authority to put me in reform school because of my religious convictions.

# 18

## "Greeny!"

The next morning I got a glimpse of Union College and heard its bell ring out a welcome. I thought, "Surely it will be wonderful to attend that school, where all are Christians!"

Of course, I did not have a cent of money with which to begin school. The money the friends in South Dakota had given me was only a few cents more than enough to pay my fare to Lincoln. I was not discouraged, however. I felt sure that God would provide. I stayed at a friend's home briefly.

At Christmastime the president of the college sent for me to come to his office. After a short visit he took me to an adjoining room where the faculty was in session and asked me to tell something of my experiences. I told a few of the most trying experiences as briefly as I could and also of my desire to obtain an education so I could be of service to the Lord.

As a result, during the vacation a place was found where I could work for room and board. The faculty made arrangements for me to attend college the remainder of the year at no cost.

I thought that the few pieces of clothing I had received from different ones would enable me to attend school. One of the teachers helped find inexpensive secondhand textbooks. I was never so happy as on the morning I began school. I thought that all trials were past. Every faculty member appeared faultless to me; even the students seemed to be almost perfect. School life promised to be wonderful. Daily I thanked God for the privilege of attending a Christian school.

This peace did not last long, however. Satan had tried to discourage me in many ways before this but had not succeeded. When he saw I was getting on so well, he evidently decided to bring his forces against me from another angle. He found someone in the Christian school through whom he could work.

One day as I sat in chapel, a note was handed me. The message it conveyed was anything but kind, reference being made to my poor clothing. I put the note in my book. I felt terribly hurt. I did not dare to look around to see if I could locate the writer. I did not say a word to anyone, but I kept the note. During much of the night I wept. I was homesick for my loved ones, and this unkind note weighed heavily upon me. I had a real battle to make myself return to school the next morning. I knew I did not have pretty silk and velvet dresses as some of the students had. But what I had was clean; so I had been content. I wished I had clothes from home; but wishing did not help me any. There was no chance of getting them.

The next few days things went smoothly again. I forgot my troubles and began to enjoy my schoolwork; but Satan was still on my track. About two weeks later I received another note during chapel. It said, "Say you, Greeny! You had better get some different clothes if you want to attend college. (Signed) Ha! Ha!"

This note made me feel even worse than the first. I quickly put it in my book so that no one would see it. One good woman had given me a dark-green skirt and another had given me a blouse to match. These were the only clothes I had besides the few working clothes others had given me.

Some of the girls had a change for each day of the week and

two or three changes for Sabbath and evening entertainments. I became very much discouraged and conscious of my clothing. I thought it would be better to quit school and work for a while in order to get some better clothes. It was hard to keep my mind on my studies.

Near noon I had a study period; so I went back to my chapel seat, where I had left some of my books. As I entered, I noticed two girls whispering and laughing. One of them said, "You could stand some new shoes, couldn't you?" Then they laughed. I sat down in my seat, but I could not study. My heart was pressing up into my throat, so I took my books and went home.

Knowing my school program, the lady where I stayed inquired, "Why, what is wrong, Helen? Why are you home at this hour?"

"Nothing is wrong," I answered, and hurried to my room, where I changed my clothes and got ready for work.

When I came out, she said, "Don't you have a class the last period today?"

"Yes, ma'am," I replied.

"Then why aren't you attending it?"

In spite of the battle to cover my feelings, the tears came. This dear mother in Israel knew something was wrong, so she said, "Come over here, dear, and sit down beside me and tell me what is troubling you. Are you homesick, or are you discouraged with your schoolwork?"

Upon her insistence to know what the trouble was, I showed her the notes I had received. She was amazed, and said, "I know this hurts you, Helen, but remember, the ones who wrote these notes are not Christians. No Christian student would treat a poor fellow student that way.

I was quite surprised to hear her say that, for I had the idea that everyone in school was a genuine follower of Christ.

In the evening I told her that I had just about decided to stay out of school and earn some money for new clothes. She said, "That will not do! You are going back to school in the morning."

79

I dreaded to go back wearing that green dress for fear they would call me "greeny" again, and my shoes were badly worn. My stockings were getting so bad that they would not stay whole, no matter how I mended them. So all in all, I thought I had sufficient reason to stop attending school for a while.

In the morning I left for school at the regular hour. But instead of going to classes, I went to another friend's home. I told her my plans, but she insisted, too, that I go back to school, which I did. One of the professors met me in the hall and asked me why I was not in my last class the day before, or in my first class that morning. I told him I could not come. He said, "I understand why you did not come. I am glad you are back now. The woman you work for called and told about the embarrassment you have passed through. The notes you received are also in our possession. We are sorry about this. Don't let it discourage you. We will check up on these unkind deeds. Our school will not tolerate such goings on."

# 19

# God Provides

In a dream one night God spoke to one of the saintly mothers near the college. He showed her a girl in distress and poorly clad. She was so impressed with the dream that she awoke and could not sleep the rest of the night. During the day that dream kept haunting her. At last she telephoned my employer.

"I can see the girl yet," she said. "I wonder if there could be someone in such need. I would surely help if I knew. That dream follows me, no matter what I do."

My employer told her in brief how the girl who was working for her was cast out of her home when she accepted the truth. She also told her of the notes I had received, and that I was discouraged and wanted to stop school because of lack of proper clothes.

The woman, whom I had never seen and who had never seen me, replied, "Send her down to me as soon as she is through with her work today."

When I came home from school, I was told that a woman down the street had called and wished me to come see her. I had no idea what the stranger might want, but I went. When she came to the door, she exclaimed in surprise, "Well!

Well! Here is the very girl I saw in a dream last night!" She threw her arms around me and invited me in.

After we were seated, she said, "Let me see the soles of your shoes, my dear. Now let me see your stockings." I took off my shoes and let her see them. They were patch upon patch. Tears filled her eyes as she said, "Well, I am so thankful that God directed me in a dream to help you. I saw your worn shoes and stockings and poor clothes in my dream. Come with me to my bedroom."

She opened her wardrobe and gave me two changes of everything needed, from stockings to dresses. Then she said, "Now we are going to the store." She took me to see the storekeeper and told him how God had directed her to help me. She also told him a bit about my needs.

"I have heard about a young lady at the college who was disowned by her parents when she accepted this truth," he said. "But I do not know the girl."

"Well, this is the girl," she told him. "Can you do anything for her?"

"Yes, I surely will," he answered in his kind, friendly way. He went to the shelves and got me a fine pair of shoes and a pair of rubbers. I left that store feeling rich indeed.

Unbeknown to me, the woman with whom I lived got in touch with the Dorcas Society during the week. The next Sunday I was asked to meet with them, and they gave me a good coat and hat. The story of my experience began to spread among the church members, so various ones gave me articles of clothing. In a short time I had more clothes than I had ever before owned.

One of the students at school overheard someone telling my experience to a friend one day. This young student wrote home and told her parents about it and said she wished she could do something for the girl about whom she was writing. Her parents sent her $10 to use as she saw fit. As soon as she received it, she sat down and wrote the following words: "Therefore I say unto you, Take no thought for your life, what ye shall eat, or what ye shall drink; nor yet for your body, what ye shall put on. Is not the life more than meat, and the body than raiment? Behold the fowls of the air: for they sow not, neither do they reap, nor gather into barns; yet your heavenly Father feedeth them. Are ye not much better than they? . . . And why take ye thought for raiment? Consider the lilies of the field, how they grow; they toil not, neither do they spin: and yet I say unto you, That even Solomon in all his glory was not arrayed like one of these. . . . Therefore take no thought, saying, What shall we eat? or, What shall we drink? or, Wherewithal shall we be clothed? . . . But seek ye first the kingdom of God, and His righteousness; and all these things shall be added unto you." Matthew 6:25-33.

With that beautiful text she placed the $10 in an envelope, on which she wrote my name. Underneath it were these words: "God knew your needs. (Signed) Yours with Christian love."

When I came home and found this letter on my table with the money, I felt sure an angel had visited my room. I had been penniless for months. I had been well provided with clothing, but I had no cash to buy stamps, pencils, paper, and other things, and every Sabbath I felt pained and embarrassed because I had no money to put in the offering. I at once paid one dollar tithe and another dollar as a thank offering.

School would close shortly, and I was casting about as to what I should do during the summer. I decided to enter the colporteur work and sell *Daniel and the Revelation.*

As I began canvassing immediately after the close of school, I prayed God to help me exert the same courteous and uplifting influence on the people I should meet as did that friendly man who sold father his first Adventist book—the very one I was now going to sell.

I had worked hard all one day to finish canvassing a little town. I sold only one small book, *Best Stories,* but had not secured a single order for the large book. I finished the town about four o'clock, with just enough money to purchase a ticket to the next place. I arrived there about five o'clock. This was quite a large city. I walked up the main business section to get an idea of where I wished to begin my work.

I was somewhat uneasy, for I had had no success during the day. Now I was penniless in a strange city. The question kept thrusting itself into the foreground, "Where will you sleep tonight? and where will you get your supper and breakfast?" until I almost became frightened. I decided I would work hard until suppertime, hoping I could sell enough small books to help me get a place to stay that night. I worked hard until ten minutes to six and received nothing but the coldest treatment. I had not sold a single help, to say nothing of taking an order for the large book.

It made me hungry to smell supper cooking in the different homes. Some of the women were really cross when they came to the door, because they were interrupted so near their mealtime. One lady who was especially cross asked me if I had a permit to sell books in the city. I told her I had not secured any thus far, because no one had asked me for one. She said, "My husband is on the police force. How would you like it if he stopped you?" Then she slammed the door. I was almost too discouraged to go any farther, when in the next block I saw a bridge spanning a running stream. I walked over and watched the water running along peacefully. Then I walked down the street about a block until I could get courage to begin again.

I went back to where I left off, but again my courage sank. I knew people would be eating supper now, and I would be even less welcome than a few minutes before. So I thought I would pass the supper hour walking along the stream and return to my work after the people had eaten and were in a better mood. It seemed that my stomach had never been so empty as it was right then, when I did not have a cent to purchase anything to eat. Suddenly I heard the voices of some children. They were coming toward me along the stream. I saw they each had a pail, and as they came near, I could see that these pails were filled with strawberries. One little girl questioned, "Are you going to get strawberries, too?"

I said, "Maybe I will, if there are any left."

The children all shouted, "Oh, there are a lot of them left just a little way beyond that tall tree that is hanging over the water!" I thanked them and walked on toward the spot.

What a feast I had! I ate all I wanted and thanked God for providing such a delicious free supper for me. After washing my hands in the stream, I hurried back to put in a little more time at my work. I was hoping I could sell something to pay for a night's lodging.

Near the bridge I had to pass a large white house.
As I looked, I saw a lady sitting alone on the porch weeping. I felt impressed to stop and talk to her. Following my inclination, I started up the walk toward her home. She tried to brush aside her tears as she unhooked the screen door to let me in. She seemed to be a very fine woman, and I felt at home with her the minute I entered. She opened her heart and told me of losing her husband only two years before. Another deep sorrow had recently come to her home. Her only daughter had died two weeks before I came. She said, "As I saw you coming along the stream, I thought you walked so much like my dear girl. As you came closer, you looked so much like her that I just couldn't keep back the tears. I wished you would turn in so I could find out who you are and where you live."

"I am a stranger in this city," I told her, "and was just looking for a place to stay for the night."

"What do you plan to do in town?" she asked in a kind manner.

Then I told her of my work selling Christian literature and my purpose to help people. The tears rolled down her cheeks all during the time I showed her the large book. She gave her order for *Daniel and the Revelation* and for four *Best Stories*. I thanked her for the order and was getting ready to leave when she said, "I am sure God sent you here. You have been a blessing to me. Won't you stay with me tonight?"

We spent a happy evening together. Before we retired, I asked her if she would object if I read a portion of God's Word.

85

Then we would have prayer together. She exclaimed, "I think that would be wonderful!" I read the Beatitudes (Matthew 5:3-9) and part of Revelation 21:1-7: "And I saw a new heaven and a new earth: for the first heaven and the first earth were passed away; and there was no more sea. . . . And God shall wipe away all tears from their eyes; and there shall be no more death, neither sorrow, nor crying, neither shall there be any more pain: for the former things are passed away. . . . He that overcometh shall inherit all things; and I will be his God, and he shall be My son."

I also read the words of the beautiful song, "The Lord Knows Why," which I had written in the back of my Bible. This song had been a great comfort to me and I hoped it would console her.

I may not know the reason why
Dark clouds so often veil the sky;
But, though my sea be smooth or rough,
The Lord knows why, and that's enough.

I may not know why I am led
So often in the paths I dread;
But, trusting Him, I'll press my way.
The Lord knows why; I will obey.

I may not know why death should come
To take the dear ones from my home;
But, though mine eyes with tears be dim,
The Lord knows why; I'll trust in Him.

So, though I may not understand
The leadings of my Father's hand,
I know to all He has the key;
He understands each mystery.

Oh yes, He knows. The Lord knows why
These things are ordered from on high;
And, though dark clouds may hide the sun,
The Lord knows why—His will be done.

After I finished reading, she said, "Read it again!" I read it the second time. Then we knelt and had prayer. She took me to my room, and how good the clean bed looked to me.

The next morning as I walked up the street to begin my work, I suddenly felt a strong hand take hold of my shoulder. I was rather startled as I looked up into the face of a big policeman. He was pleasant, however. He asked about my work, whereupon I turned right around and gave him a canvass for my book. But he did not appear much interested.

After I had finished, he asked, "Who gave you permission to sell books like that?"

"The Lord said we should go to all the world and carry the gospel to the people," I told him. "This town is a part of this world, and I am endeavoring to fulfill the Lord's commission."

He stood silent, so I said, "Shall I read it to you?"

"What would you read it from?" he asked.

"The Bible," I said.

"All right, read it," he answered.

I quickly pulled out my Bible, which I always carried with me in my prospectus bag. I read the text that came to my mind first, Mark 16:15: "And He said unto them, Go ye into all the world, and preach the gospel to every creature."

He smiled and patted me on the shoulder as he said, "You're all right! Put me down for a book in the leather binding. If anyone troubles you about a permit, call me!" He handed me his card and left.

For five weeks I worked in that city. I had no more trouble about a permit, and I stayed at my new friend's home the entire time at no cost. She had six young ladies rooming and boarding with her; so I helped her with the morning and evening work. She appreciated this, and I was indeed grateful for her hospitality.

# 20

## The Classroom Lie

The first period of the new school year was over, and examinations were on. One morning in an oral test the teacher directed a question to a young woman who sat right behind me. She did not answer it correctly, and so the teacher put the question to me. This delay had given me time to think about it; therefore I was able to answer correctly.

This angered the girl, who, in order to revenge herself, wrote a note and sent it to the teacher. In it she accused me of cheating, claiming that I had read the answer from my textbook.

When he dismissed the class, the teacher asked me to stay. He closed the door and then reprimanded me severely. For a while I sat silent, wondering what I could have done. Finally I said, "May I ask why I am being thus reproved?" He then showed me the note. I said, "I have no way to prove that I am not guilty of the accusation. I can only say I am innocent and ask you to take my word."

He replied, "I will try to find the writer of the note, and let you face whoever it may be." Then he excused me.

I felt terrible! It was such a shock that I cried all the way home. I told the lady for whom I worked about the humiliating experience, and she pleaded, "Don't feel so bad about it, dear; just keep your chin up. The one who told the lie will be revealed sometime."

By the next morning the teacher had compared the handwriting of the note with the essays he had on his desk and had found the writer. He asked us both to stay after class. I was surprised and grieved when I saw the pretty, well-dressed girl who was guilty. I could scarcely think she could be so unkind.

The teacher asked me, "Do you still maintain that you are not guilty of the charges of this note?"

"I can truthfully say I am not guilty," I replied.

Then he turned to the other girl and said, "What made you say on the note that this student cheated? Did you see her?"

"I did!" she affirmed.

"Are you sure?" the teacher asked again.

"I am sure!" she said.

He excused her then and talked to me. I knew I could not say more than I had the day before, and there was no way to make him believe me any more than he believed the other girl. Therefore, I kept silent. It was a bitter trial for me to bear this reproach. It hung over me like a dark cloud for many days. I felt too mortified to face my teacher. I was horrified at the thought of what the rest of the faculty would think of me when they heard about it.

One day I met the girl on the street alone, and I asked her why she had brought that false accusation against me. She retorted, "It made me mad because you thought you were so smart, and answered that question so quickly. You should have waited until I at least had a second chance. You didn't, so I thought I would make it hot for you."

"Well," I replied, "will you make that statement in the presence of the teacher?"

She turned and said, "If you tell this to the teacher, I will tell him you not only cheated but that you also made up this lie." Then she hastened away, laughing.

A few days later I missed the girl from class. Questioning

89

one of my friends from the dormitory, I learned that she was very ill and that the doctor had been to see her twice a day the last few days. Many thoughts went through my mind. I thought how terrible it would be if the girl should die with that lie unforgiven. I went to the greenhouse and bought a pretty little bouquet of flowers and sent them to her by her roommate. A few days later I was handed an envelope containing a sincere apology for the wrong she had done.

The next morning when I went to class, my teacher reached out and shook my hand. "I humbly ask your forgiveness for not taking your word the other day," he said, "and for giving you such a stern reproof without being sure of my ground. Look at this note. The girl has written a confession which vindicates you. I am sorry I caused you grief so unjustly."

Then he added, "This surely was an unfortunate experience. But don't be discouraged, for you are clear now. I would much rather have had your experience, even if it was hard, than that of the other student."

"Come, go for a walk with me," this girl told me as soon as she was strong enough to return to school. On the way she asked, "Can you forgive me for the awful thing I did to you, Helen? I felt terribly condemned when I received the flowers you sent me, and I saw my cruelty."

"I have already forgiven you," I said. "I am not holding anything against you."

"I am the only child in our family, and have always had everything I wanted," she said with tears. "I was always told that I was smarter than others, and that I was all right, no matter what I did. So I grew up to be very selfish. I never could stand to have anyone get ahead of me. If anyone did, I would make it difficult for him. That is why I did this wicked thing to you. I am grown-up now and should know better. But it is terribly hard to correct these lifelong habits. Sometimes I feel very bad because my parents let me grow up like this without correcting my faults."

Poor girl! I felt sorry for her, for she had much to endure in order to remove those selfish traits of character from her life. I was thankful that with all the difficulties I had suffered at home, our parents had taught us to give and take, to rejoice in others' victories and to sympathize in their defeats. They also taught us that good looks are not the things that make us count in this world but that good behavior, discretion, sincerity, and honesty are the attributes that are pleasing to God and man.

# 21

## My Visit Home

I wrote letters home regularly, although I never received a reply. Father always saw to it that he called for the mail, and he did not let the rest of the family know he had heard from me. Mother and my brothers and sisters were worrying about how and where I might be.

Sister Katie happened to be in town one day, and so she called for the mail. To her surprise the postmaster handed her a letter from me. She answered it right away and got it in the mail before she returned home. How happy I was! I answered it immediately, but father received my reply and knew from it that Katie had written to me. Whereupon he wrote a very strong letter, informing me that my name was erased from the family record. I was no longer to call myself a member of his family. He asked me not to write home again.

Katie waited for some time for an answer. When it failed to come, she thought father might be keeping her letters. She wrote again and asked me to address her in care of a neighbor. I was glad for this suggestion. Now I could keep in touch with her and other members of the family. These letters helped to break the awful loneliness I felt at times during the four years that elapsed before I saw my family again.

Father seemed to have bad luck in whatever he undertook, and one accident after another befell the family. One autumn day my sixteen-year-old sister, Lydia, was working in a cornfield when some hunters came by and shot into the field. The whole charge struck her in the face, and she lost both of her eyes. This was a terrible blow for the family.

Sister was sad and despondent. She suffered intense pain for months. She often asked our parents to let me come home that I might talk to her; but father denied her the privilege.

One day father became ill. The doctor told him he had better set his house in order, for death might call at any time. He was quiet for some time. Mother saw he was having a real battle about something. Finally he called her to the bed and said, "Maybe we had better let Helen come home." Sister Katie hurried to send the message for me to come.

I took the first train home and arrived late the next night. Good old Fido was the first to greet me. He knew me and barked and danced with delight. After petting him, I walked up to the house and knocked. Mother came to the door. After greetings were over, she took me to father's room. By the time I reached home he was so much better that he was not so anxious to see me as he had been. He feared I might influence members of the family to follow in my footsteps, and so he was cold toward me. I sat down beside his bed, however, and talked to him and stroked his toilworn hands for a while. I loved him even if he had treated me roughly. Then I went upstairs.

After I had greeted the other members of the family, mother took me to my blind sister's room. It was almost more than I could bear to see what a terrible calamity had come to my youngest sister and how it had changed her looks. She cried bitterly when she put her arms around my neck and said, "I can never see you again in this world." I got into bed with her and we visited until near morning. I told her what a comfort this blessed truth had been to me.

She said, "I often thought there really must be something in the Adventist message because you were willing to go through so much in order to live it. I often asked the folks to let you come home so that I could talk to you; but it took until now." I told her about the blessed hope of our Lord's return and other points of our faith. Her heart began to reach out for Jesus to come into her life.

Things went along well until the next forenoon when our rough neighbor and my cousin John arrived. The minute the neighbor saw me, he started trouble. He made many threatening remarks, and I listened to him for a while. I would have taken all this abuse had it come from a member of my family; but I thought it was cowardly to sit and take it from him. He had no right to say anything, and I finally said, "Sir, do you know that we live in a land of religious liberty?" At this the man flew into a rage and said he just ached to lay his hands on me.

John called to him, "Old fellow, you'd better keep your hands off her! Just one slap may take your whole farm." This made him angry at cousin John, and he started on him.

After arguing with John awhile, he left him and came back at me. It seemed the only way he could get his revenge was to point to the large family record that hung in the living room. Gritting his teeth while pointing to the record, he said, "Now to whose family do you belong? And who will give you your property when you get married?" Then he laughed loudly.

When I looked at the record and saw my name crossed out with black ink, a strange feeling came over me. I turned about and looked at father. He was looking down. I said, "Father, that is quite all right. I love you anyway, and I am still of your flesh and blood even if my name is crossed out on the family record. Let me sing just one stanza of the song I often sing as a prayer:

> "Lord, I care not for riches, neither silver nor gold;
> I would make sure of heaven, I would enter the fold;
> In the book of Thy kingdom, with its pages so fair,
> Tell me, Jesus, my Saviour, is my name written there?"

When I turned about, the neighbor was gone. Mother said he put his hands over his ears and ran out when I began to sing. I was glad he was gone.

When father noticed that all my brothers and sisters gathered closely around me, he said, "You had better go back to your school, Helen. I am afraid your Adventist influence around here is not for the upbuilding of our home. You had better go." I knew I must obey, for father always meant what he said. As I looked around, everyone stood quietly, and my blind sister began to sob. My heart ached for the poor girl. She could hardly bear the terrible darkness into which she had been plunged. She knew her life would indeed be dreary, and she longed for spiritual sight that would pierce the dark future.

I took her by the hand and went upstairs. I quickly read Isaiah 35 to her. She rejoiced especially over verses 3-6, and 10: "Strengthen ye the weak hands, and confirm the feeble knees. Say to them that are of a fearful heart, Be strong, fear not: behold, your God will come with vengeance, even God with a recompense; He will come and save you. Then the eyes of the blind shall be opened, and the ears of the deaf shall be un- stopped. Then shall the lame man leap as an hart, and the tongue of the dumb sing: for in the wilderness shall waters break out, and streams in the desert." "And the ransomed of the Lord shall return, and come to Zion with songs and ever- lasting joy upon their heads: they shall obtain joy and gladness, and sorrow and sighing shall flee away."

I kissed her Good-bye and assured her that I would make a real effort to get her into a school for the blind. Then I hurried downstairs and said Good-bye to the others. Dear old grandpa was there, too. He slipped a few dollars into my hand as he bade me Good-bye, bless his heart!

As I went out the door, I begged once more that my parents be sure to send Lydia to the school for the blind; but they did not feel that they could let her go away from home in her sad condition.

My eldest sister was married soon after this visit, and Lydia went to stay with her. Together we made arrangements to send her to the school for the blind in Gary, South Dakota. She took music and learned to play many hymns, which proved a real comfort to her. She learned to knit, crochet, weave rugs, and read and write in Braille.

She often said after she took her stand for the truth, "Even though I am blind, yet this truth forms a ray of light that shines through to the end of time." Her favorite song, "Lead Kindly Light," sustains her.

After leaving college, I entered the nurse's training course. I worked in a doctor's office for some time after becoming a graduate nurse. Then I accepted a call from the South Dakota Conference to help in evangelistic tent meetings in that state. I joined some of the very people who had held the tent meetings in my hometown years before. Once more I saw the organ the persecutors had to buy for the ministers. What a privilege it was to fill the same place in a series of tent meetings that those dear people filled at the time when my heart was drawn to God!

We located in a wicked town. Attendance at the effort was good, but we received threats all the while. It was a terribly hot summer, with no rain for weeks. A man who claimed he was God lived in that community. He kept telling people that he would not let a drop of rain fall until that "idol temple" (our tent) was burned down. He had many friends possessed of the same spirit as he. The young man who was tent master for us had to be on guard all the while. But, in spite of his watchfulness, our tent burned one night with the organ, songbooks, seats, and all.

The minister who was leading the meetings was a man of courage; so the next morning he and the young tent master went uptown and rented the town hall, where we continued the meetings. The summer passed, and not a drop of rain came even after our tent was burned. People kept teasing this man, who claimed he was God, saying, "You said you would give rain after the 'idol temple' was burned. Where is your rain?"

Mr. Oswald, the tent master, and I became friends during these meetings and carried on correspondence after he returned to college. During the school year I had the pleasant task of being matron at South Dakota Academy. In the summer Mr. Oswald and I were together in another series of meetings. In the fall I returned to my work in the doctor's office.

During the winter my brother, Leonhard, accepted the truth and came to live with me. We rented a room and did light housekeeping. We greatly enjoyed being together.

In the spring Mr. Oswald and I were married. The leading minister had been assigned to a foreign mission field; so my husband had to take the leadership of the meetings, which started five days after our wedding. Our wedding trip consisted of a long trek across the country by team and wagon to the place where the meetings were to be conducted.

# 22

# The House Burns Down

While I was still attending college and soon after my visit home, father became very discouraged because of all the accidents and calamities that seemed to be following him. So he sold the home and moved to Canada, hoping that things would be better in a new country.

Moving from the prairies of South Dakota into a heavily timbered section of Alberta was indeed a change for father and mother. They found that clearing timber was almost harder work than removing stones from their South Dakota land had been. However, the whole family got under the load, and before many months passed, a number of fields were ready for planting. There was much other hard work in starting the new farm, as only those can understand who have done it. A new house and other buildings were to be built. Some of the smaller buildings were made from logs, but the house, a comfortable two-story building, was erected with good lumber.

The bad luck and the heartaches of the former home were somewhat forgotten. Lydia returned home after spending a number of years at Gary. In spite of her blindness, she was now able to play and sing and to work with her hands. She spread much sunshine in the home.

About four o'clock one cold morning mother was awakened by the smell of smoke which seemed to be filling the rooms. She quickly aroused the family, and they barely escaped with their lives. Father tried to get a few things out before the flames enveloped them, but his efforts were in vain. He was the last one to get out of the burning building. As he ran out of the door, he heard something drop and felt it fall against his heels. He looked around to see what it might be and was surprised to find his Bible following him. He picked it up and held it under his arm as they stood there that dark, cold night watching the flames consume their comfortable home.

Father wrote to me the next day and told about the fire that had destroyed their home. He said, "The only thing we saved besides ourselves was the Bible you sent to me for a birthday present a few years ago. Just why this Bible followed me I do not know. I kept it on a little shelf near the door. When I left the house, it fell out after me."

I sent my parents a telegram as soon as I received the letter and assured them that Leonhard and I would send money at once. Leonhard had some money saved, and I had some due me from nursing. Together we had a good check to send. In the letter that accompanied it we told our parents that we were also sending a box by express.

We gathered together everything we could spare and obtained some things from friends and neighbors to put in the box. It contained almost everything, from quilts, blankets, and pillows to kitchen utensils. Father wrote and expressed appreciation for the help. In conclusion he said, "I only wish I could have saved my watch. I feel lost without it." Later Leonhard and I managed to buy him a good watch, which pleased him greatly.

The house was insured, and my parents had no trouble getting it rebuilt. One day the neighbors for miles around came with teams and helped get the lumber and build the new house. With many hands the work went quickly, and soon they had a good home again. The spring work started shortly after the house was completed, and Leonhard went home to help put in a big crop. God blessed it, and it looked as if it would yield a hundredfold.

Near harvesttime Leonhard wrote, "We expect to start harvesting a heavy crop in a few days. Father is sick and mother is overworked. Pack your grip and bring your babies (I had two small children at this time), and come out and help mother during harvesting and threshing. We will help with the fare."

I was happy for this opportunity of seeing my parents again.

We arrived in the evening. Father was suffering severely from rheumatism; so I put the children to bed and made ready to treat his swollen knees and ankles. As I proceeded with the treatment, he said, "This makes me think of the time years ago when I was bedfast for weeks with this same trouble and you took care of me nights." I was glad he had not forgotten our previous companionship.

In the morning he told me that the treatments relieved him so much that he had had the first good night's rest in three weeks. After breakfast he became acquainted with his new grandchildren and took a real liking to them. They recited their memory verses and sang their little Sabbath school songs for him, which he enjoyed.

He responded well to the treatments, and was soon able to be out and help with some of the work. By the time threshing started, he was himself again and did much of the heavy work.

In the middle of the afternoon of the first day of threshing I said, "Mother, I am going to fix some sliced peaches with cream and a glass of lemonade and a few cookies to take out to father." She cheerfully consented. When I arrived with the lunch, he gladly took it and sat down on the side of the wagon box to rest while he ate. I tried to shovel off some of the wheat for him, but I had not done any work of that kind for some years. Consequently, my muscles were not equal to the heavy task. Father laughed at my efforts. After he finished the lunch, he handed me the dishes with the words, "Thank you, my child; that was refreshing." It seemed so good to hear father address me as his child again that I could not hold back the tears.

"What is wrong?" mother asked me when I reached the house.

"Nothing is wrong, mother," I replied. "I can see that everything is going to be all right. Father called me his child once more as he used to before I became an Adventist."

"Yes," said mother, "the old family record on which your name was crossed out was burned with the house; now we can make a new one. On it your name should be written in letters of gold because you had to break the hard soil all alone years ago. Had you not been faithful to God's calling, we might all be in darkness yet. As it is, most of us are on the road toward the kingdom with you. I hope I, too, can soon keep the Sabbath and be baptized."

Only those who have experienced the thrill of seeing an answer to prayer that has ascended for long years can know the joy that filled my heart at that moment. Mother and I both shed tears of happiness.

One noon father said, "I will not be home for supper with the crew. I plan to take two or three loads of grain to the elevator in order to get some cash to pay our help when we get through threshing." It was sometime after dark when his last load was taken to the elevator. He received $84.75 for his wheat. The seventy-five cents change he put in his overalls pocket. The $84 was all paper money, which he rolled up intending to put it in a trousers pocket underneath his overalls. But he happened to put it between the overalls and his trousers. Fortunately he got on his wagon immediately and drove home. When he reached home, the gate to the yard was closed. He jumped off and opened the gate, then drove in and took care of his team. The tired threshers had all gone to rest by this time. Father was very tired, too, so he ate a bit of supper and went to bed.

The next morning they began threshing very early, so that

they would get through by noon. Mother, Lydia, my children, and I were the only ones at home. The old dog was lying by the gate sunning himself. As they ran down there to play with him, the children found father's roll of money. They, of course, did not know what it was. They liked very much to cut out pictures; so when they saw all those "faces," they decided to come to the house and cut them out. My little girl picked up her dress, forming a basket, and her brother gathered all the "green pictures" (as they called them) and filled the basket; then they started toward the house.

After giving me the flowers they had picked on the way to the house, they asked for the scissors.

"What do you want them for?" I inquired.

"We found a lot of pictures at the gate," they told me, "and we want to cut them out."

"Where are the pictures?" I asked.

My little girl then dropped her dress and out rolled various denominations of bills. Mother and I could not understand why they should have found all that money at the gate, as they said.

We had counted $76, when we heard father enter, all exhausted. He had noticed his money was gone and had hurried home to see if it might have fallen out in the bedroom when he undressed the night before. When he saw the money, he said, "Oh, I am so glad I lost it in the house! How much have you?"

We gave him the amount.

"But, grandpa," my little boy broke in, "we found that at the gate."

Father was amazed and said, "I must have put it between my pockets. Evidently it dropped out when I jumped off the wagon to open the gate last evening. I wonder where the rest is. I had $84 rolled up together."

We all hurried to the place where the children said they had found the money. After searching awhile, father found two more dollars near the stream that ran through a corner of the yard near the gate. Because there was a strong northwest wind blowing, father thought the rest had been blown into the stream and carried away. We were glad that at least $78 of this hard-earned money was recovered. After father was gone, the children and I went back to see if we could possibly find some more. We found $4 at the edge of the water, caught on some weeds. As a reward, father gave each of the children $2, and also bought a new cap for the boy and new shoes for the little girl.

After threshing was finished, we got ready to start home. Mother was not feeling well the day we left; so father took us to the train alone. When he said Good-bye, he put a new bill in my hand. He clasped his grandchildren tightly as the train pulled up to the station. Soon we were seated in the coach. Dear old father stood by the window. I reached out and held on to his toilworn hands. He tried to smile as the children kept saying, "Good-bye, grandpa. I love you."

Soon the conductor called, "All aboard!" Father looked up at us once more and said Good-bye. His eyes were filled with tears. Somehow I felt he wanted to say something that was on his heart, but he could not.

The latter part of January that winter I received a letter from mother. "I have taken my stand for the truth and have begun the new year right," she wrote. "Also two of the younger boys are taking their stand with me. Father is very much displeased and is talking some of leaving home. He has threatened to take Reuben [the youngest boy] with him, so that he will not become an Adventist also." She closed by saying, "Pray that God may not permit that to happen, for I could not stand to have my baby boy taken from me."

# 23

# Father Leaves Home

Thinking that he would be happier alone than with his family, who were keeping the Sabbath, father left home one morning. He was gone about three days. Then he returned to pack a few things.

"Where are you going?" mother asked him as he put some bedding, dishes, and other household furnishings on the wagon.

"I have bought a place about nine miles from here," he answered. "It is away out in the woods where no Adventist will be around! Get Reuben's clothes ready, for I am going to take him along."

"I don't want to go with father!" Reuben cried.

"Oh, but you must go if father tells you to," mother comforted him. Much against her desire she packed his clothes, feeling sure that father would not stay away long. She also packed a big box of food for them.

What a sad picture! Father driving away with a few pieces of furniture and the youngest child on the wagon!

After they had been gone a number of days, mother baked a batch of cookies and some fresh bread. "I think I'll take some cookies and bread to father if we can find him," she said. "I shall also cook some food I know he especially likes."

With the food and three of the boys, mother drove away into the woods to find father's new home. They had a hard time finding it because there was hardly a road leading into the thick woods where he lived. Reuben cried for joy when he saw his mother and brothers. "I have been so lonesome!" he wept. Father was lonely, too, but he would not admit it to them.

Week after week passed, and he remained on his place. About twice a week mother would send over supplies of food and clean clothes. She and other members of the family begged him to come home, but he refused.

Life finally became so monotonous for him that he decided to take a trip. He and Reuben traveled to the eastern part of the United States, hoping to find contentment. But they knew no one anywhere and were very lonely. Because Reuben was so homesick and because they found Adventists in the East also, they returned after a few weeks' absence.

The second day of father's homeward trip a minister boarded the train. He saw that father appeared sad and lonely. After watching him, he decided to join father and visit with him. He stepped over and introduced himself. Father at once made room for him to sit down. The minister opened the conversation by saying, "I see, sir, that you are rather sad, and that you are traveling alone with the boy. I take it for granted that your wife is either sick in a hospital or has died."

Father was rather touched by his sympathetic remarks, and tears came to his eyes. The minister felt sure that the little boy's mother must have died, and he tried to give comfort.

Father finally said, "I have lost not only my wife but also most of my children."

The minister was almost taken off his feet. "Tell me what great calamity has come to you," he begged.

"A number of years ago," father began, "the Seventh-day Adventists came to our hometown and sowed their seed. As a result, one of my children became a Jew, and one after another the other members of my family began to take up with their doctrines, until now my wife has begun to keep the Sabbath!"

"That surely is unfortuante!" the minister said. "Those Adventists should all be imprisoned or sent to some island where they cannot spread their propaganda. They are nothing more than false prophets! If they want church members so much, why don't they go and convert the heathen? Instead, they insist on going about breaking up the peace in our churches."

Turning to father, the minister asked, "By the way, to what church do you belong?"

"To none at the present time," father answered.

Surprised, the minister said, "May I ask why?"

"Because none of the denominations live up to the Bible," father retorted.

They contended for a while, the minister claiming they did and father trying to prove that they did not. Indignant, the minister exclaimed, "I am not at all surprised that your family joined those crooked Adventists! You are not straight yourself!"

By this time father was getting angry, and he pointed a finger at the minister and said, "You may call the Adventists crooked; but, let me tell you, they are straighter than other churches are, including yours! At least they live what they preach, and they have Bible proof for most of their doctrine!"

At this the minister rose and went to the smoker. A passenger who sat in a seat just ahead of father had overheard their argument. This man turned about and took up the conversation with father.

"I listened in on your conversation, sir," he said. "It was interesting, indeed. I think you have much for which to be thankful in having your family turn to religion. I would thank God a thousand times if my family had any inclination to serve God; but they despise religion."

Here he paused a moment and breathed a deep sigh. "My wife," he proceeded, "became interested in things outside the family when the children were small, which proved a detriment

106

to our home. She was gone for hours, and the children were left unsupervised, often until the late hours of the night. No one knew where she was. I was out on the road much of the time, as I am now, to make the living for the family. Therefore I could not spend much time with the children and care for them. As a result, my oldest son, who was a very dear boy when small, is now in the penitentiary."

Tears began to roll down his careworn face as he continued his sad story. "My oldest girl made a shipwreck of her life and is following in her mother's footsteps. The two younger ones, a boy and a girl, are staying with relatives. Life has been hard to endure the last few years.

"I just came back from visiting my son at the penitentiary. He has been there over two years. He is despondent and begs me to get him out; but I am helpless, for I cannot get him out, no matter how much he pleads and weeps. Don't feel unhappy if your family became Seventh-day Adventists. They are good, honest people. I know them well."

Father could see that he truly was blessed; but he had not considered it so before. He tried to speak comfort to his sad seatmate. Before the man left him, father said, "Yes, I guess I should really be thankful, for I have a good, faithful wife. We reared nine boys and four girls, not one of whom smokes or drinks or plays cards. Two of my daughters married good, honest farmers. One married an Adventist minister, while the youngest is a fine Christian girl at home."

Here the station was announced at which the man had to get off.

Father was in perplexity the rest of the way, for he felt he should go home. But somehow he did not gain the victory. Reuben was so homesick that father had to let him go home when they arrived at the station. He went back to his lonely abode by himself. At times he came home to get supplies, and mother always gave him the best she had, asking him each time to come back home. He seemed to be having a terrible battle within, but each time he returned to his lonely dwelling.

Reuben told of father's visit with the two men on the train, but father never mentioned it. Reuben's story gave us new hope. We kept praying for father, for we knew he wanted to do right and that he was lonely.

One day I received the following letter from him:

"Dear Daughter:

"Your letter of recent date was greatly appreciated. It had been over at mother's for a few days before I got it. I was laid up with a sore foot, so did not get over for my supplies on the day I usually go.

"I wish to thank you, my child, for the good wishes you expressed for me. I have only good wishes for my family. What shall I write to you? I am here all alone; each day is the same. Each night I wet my pillow with tears. If the family would have stayed in the ways I taught them, then we would still be together; but they chose to be Adventists, so that fixed a great gulf between us.

"I have comfort in only one thing, and that is when I read God's Word. I read my Bible daily and weep often in my loneliness. I see now that my Bible was saved from the fire to bring comfort to me in this trying time. At times I am thankful that none of my family has chosen to walk the ways of the wicked, even if they have departed from the things I have taught them. I am casting all my burdens on the One who understands all.

"Greet your husband and the little ones. I commit you to God and His Word.

"With love I remain

"Your Father."

I answered the letter at once and urged father to return home. Mother needed him in her declining days, and he needed mother. Further, I told him that none of us was against him but that we were all for him. "There is no gulf fixed between us from our side, and we are all praying that God will in some way bind us close together again and save us as an unbroken family," I wrote.

# 24
## Sudden Death

One day shortly after father allowed Reuben to return home, mother became very depressed. She tried to work, but somehow things did not move as they should. At noon she said to the boys, "I am uneasy about father. I think you should quit work early enough so that some of you can drive over this evening to see how he is."

She had washed and mended the clothes he had left when he was home last. By the time the boys came she had fixed up a big basket of food. After supper four of them drove away to spend the evening with father. Mother did not go along because she did not feel well enough to make the trip over the rough road through the woods.

The boys arrived at father's home before dusk. He had been lonely all day, he said, and was happy when he saw the boys. All evening they had a good visit together. Shortly after eleven Willie suggested, "Well, father, I think we had better go home."

"The evening has slipped by too fast," father said. "I must not hold you longer, but I do want to say a little more before you leave. You know I used to read everything that was sent to me which said anything against the Seventh-day Adventists.

I gained nothing by doing so. The last two months I have read nothing but the Bible. I've found that the Adventists are right after all. Christ did keep the Sabbath, and so did His disciples."

Then he told of his visit with that unfortunate father on the train and how he had begun to count his blessings after that.

The boys softly began to sing:

"When upon life's billows you are tempest tossed,
When you are discouraged, thinking all is lost,
Count your many blessings, name them one by one,
And it will surprise you what the Lord hath done."

Father tried to sing with them, but his voice broke and the tears came freely. As they sang the last stanza softly, he began to sob.

"So, amid the conflict, whether great or small,
Do not be discouraged, God is over all;
Count your many blessings, angels will attend,
Help and comfort give you to the journey's end."

For a moment all sat silent. Then father said, "I am sorry I opposed my family the way I have. I thought I was right, but I see I was wrong. I hope God will forgive me. I have made up my mind to sell my things and return home where I belong."

My brothers tried to sing father's favorite song, "Now Take My Hands and Lead Me" before they separated, but they were all very much touched by father's confession. Father tried hard to sing, but his sobs and tears would not let him. As the boys started for home, he said once more, "I am so glad you came! Good night."

The boys were happy for the good news they would be able to bring to mother. The car could not carry them home fast enough. As they were nearing home, they saw the light burning in the window. They knew mother was waiting for their return and would be anxious to know how they had found father. They drove in quietly, put the car in the garage, and then went to the house together. It was after midnight, but mother was still waiting.

When she saw the smiling faces of the boys, she said, "Tell me all about your visit and how you found father."

After they told her of father's decision, she buried her face in her apron for a while and wept. Her heart was overflowing with joy. Finally she said, "At last our prayers are answered! I am so happy! Let's fix up everything the best way we know how so that he will be happy when he comes."

The boys said they were going to do all they could to make things pleasant for father when he returned. Poor blind Lydia had been sound asleep but was awakened by the conversation. Mother went to her bed and told her the good news.

"Well, we had better all get to bed for a little rest so we shall be able to do the work we have planned," mother said. Turning to the boys once more, she said, "My heart is so filled with peace and joy that I cannot express it. I feel such rest as though I were near to God." Together they sang that comforting song mother loved so well, "There Is a Place of Quiet Rest," and then retired.

The next morning father got up to attend to his morning's work. He had walked only a short distance from the house toward the barn when he fell to the ground. A neighbor who was coming by saw him fall and ran over to help. But father was dead—heart failure. This neighbor immediately sent word to mother. The same boys who had had the pleasant visit with him the evening before drove over to bring the body home. Mother was prostrate with grief. A doctor was called, but his services were not needed. Father was laid in the family lot about a mile from home, where weeping willows shelter his grave as they do baby brother's.

Little had I thought when we said Good-bye at the train that we were so soon to lose him. Father has said his last Good-bye and his last Good-night; now we are waiting for his Good-morning on that bright resurrection day.

Father was a good, honest man and always wanted to do right; but the enemy was fighting to gain his soul. The severe struggle began when, years ago, God's servant delivered to our home that book, *Daniel and the Revelation*, bearing the gospel message for these last days.

Although father consigned the book to the attic, believing that it taught heretical doctrines, seeds of truth had been sown in the hearts of his children. These seeds have brought forth an abundant harvest.

While we were all sad that father went the way he did, yet his last words have been a great comfort to us. For some time it seemed that the enemy would gain the victory in this long and hard conflict. But, thanks to God, after all the anxious years of praying and waiting, father's prejudice was broken down, and peace came to his heart before his death.

What a joy fills our hearts as we look beyond this cruel reign of sin and death and the grave to that blessed morning when all earthly trials shall be over, where none of our motives will be misunderstood and where we shall again be united with loved ones and friends who have long been sleeping in their dusty graves.